TYING FLIES

WITH JACK DENNIS AND FRIENDS

ALL FLY & SECTION DIVIDERS ILLUSTRATED
BY MIKE STIDHAM

ALL OTHER ILLUSTRATIONS BY JEFF CURRIER

EDITED BY JOE BURKE

TYING FLIES
WITH JACK DENNIS AND FRIENDS

Published by
Snake River Books
Post Office Box 4158
275 East Broadway
Jackson, Wyoming 83001

Office 1-800-937-7309

THIRD PRINTING

ISBN 978-0-937556-01-6
ISBN 0-937556-01-7

DEDICATION

The author's wife Sandy, with New Zealand guide Barry Jaggar
and a great catch.

FOR MY WIFE SANDY

My partner in life. While many times my toughest critic, always my

most ardent supporter and best friend. For without her, there would not

be any fly tying books and a family, which I treasure the most.

FOR MY CHILDREN, BRIAN, AMY & ANN

Who over the years inherited the love of the outdoors, learned

to appreciate a good cast and a honest presentation.

Each a different personality, independent, hard working, and capable.

The kind of people you would like to share a trout stream with.

Quite frankly, the best children a man could ever have.

TABLE OF CONTENTS

TABLE OF CONTENTS

FOREWORD

Mike Lawson

One of the greatest rewards in angling is tying flies and catching fish with them. For many people the fly fishing experience is incomplete unless they are catching fish with something that came from their own fingers. The tying becomes as consuming as the fish catching. Tiers turn into recipe, material and technique junkies, always searching for better ideas. These people need fresh new books and the innovative ideas spawn yet another rush of unique patterns.

I have seen many changes in my thirty odd years of fly tying, most of them centered on recipes, materials and techniques. My first flies were crude, created after dissecting the patterns I purchased at the Mercantile in Sugar City, Idaho. The most difficult part of the task was trying to figure out how the materials I took off those flies corresponded to the fly tying supplies listed in the Herter's Catalog. I wasn't lucky enough to own a book with fly tying recipes and instructions. Any advice I received from those who knew how to tie flies was greatly appreciated.

It was evident that many other fly tiers were struggling with the same problems. Most of the fly tying literature dealt with traditional Eastern patterns. Anglers in the West used to duplicate those older flies, but most of the innovative creations in the Rocky Mountains were limited to their own areas, either intentionally or unintentionally kept within small circles of fishing friends. Information did not flow as freely within our sport then as it does now.

In 1974, Jack Dennis published his first book, *Western Trout Fly Tying Manual.* This wonderful work soon became the standard of fly tying experience excellence in our part of the country. It's hard to find a fly tier in the West who hasn't been influenced in some way by this book. Part of the reason the manual was so successful was because Jack gave credit to the many individuals who had developed successful and proven patterns. He gathered all of those scattered giants of Western fly tying. Too many previous books were written with the intent of boosting the ego or the reputation of the author. Jack Dennis never had a problem giving credit where credit was due.

Many fly tying advances took place during the decade following the first book. To meet the demand, *Western Trout Fly Tying Manual (Vol.II)* was released in 1980. Volume II took up where Volume I left off. New techniques, materials and patterns, along with the people who invented them, were introduced to an eager audience. Today both volumes of "the Manual," with over 300,000 copies in print, sit on the shelves of

FOREWORD

most fly tiers in the West (and most copies show the wear of tattered covers).

Now Jack has a new fly tying book. He is the most qualified person I know to write anything about flies. Not only is he an expert tier, but he also owns a world renowned outdoor shop in Jackson, Wyoming. He spends his entire winter traveling, conducting fly fishing seminars, speaking to fly fishing clubs and attending sport shows. The only thing Jack seems to enjoy more than fly fishing is sharing ideas with other people who fly fish. Fellow anglers seem to energize him. He feeds on their enthusiasm for fly fishing and fly ty-

ing. Nobody meets more fly tiers and glimpses more innovative fly patterns than Jack Dennis.

For the past several years Gary LaFontaine and I have traveled with Jack all over this country and Canada presenting seminars on fly fishing and fly tying (our group goes by the name, The Traveling Fly Fishermen). These trips with Jack have provided me with a unique opportunity to see him at work. He is never too busy to take time to visit with a person. He is never too tired to listen to another fishing experience or evaluate another fly pattern.

This new book will follow the tradition and format of Jack's previous accomplishments. The difference is that there are even more new fly tiers and more new patterns. The difference is that these ideas, gathered in our travels all over this country and Canada, are not just for the western angler. This volume provides something exciting for everyone, no matter where they fish for trout and no matter what their level of expertise. It delights, it informs and it reveals-- from the origin of the Serendipity (told by Joe Burke) to the fishing days with the Mutant Ninja Cicada (told by Emmett Heath), it is a spectacular gathering of the best anglers and tiers in our sport today. It is a reflection ultimately of the enthusiasm of Jack Dennis - and that is the finest compliment that I can give any book.

Mike Lawson

PREFACE

Jack Dennis

For as long as I can remember, I have known fly fishing. My life is woven with memories of crisp mornings, bright waters and the wonder and excitement of fish taking a fly. My memories are a tapestry woven from solitary hours hunched over a vise, the discovery of new places and warm conversations with fishing friends, old and new. Every year I grow to love the sport more for I have learned that fly tying and fly fishing is an art, not a science.

Without a doubt there are many scientific aspects to the sport and we continue to learn and catalog this knowledge in books and videos. But it is the mystery that brings us back to the to the vise and the water. It is the fly tier's art that attempts to probe the primitive instincts of the trout. Fortunately, I'm not a deep enough thinker to spend much time trying to contemplate the psychological ramifications of trying to communicate with a creature who's brain activity may be about as sophisticated as a nervous twitch. There is still enough of the Sixties left in me to say simply, "If it feels good, do it." So I continue to tie flies and try to entice trout with this artful deceit. And so, fortunately, do many others.

It is from these many others that I have learned new aspects of the fly tier's art. I have been fortunate to learn from the best. I have gathered techniques, tools and expertise from a group as diverse as the fly fishing community itself. From professional guides like Emmett Heath, Guy Turck, and Jay Buchner to shop owners like Jim Jones, Randall Kaufmann and Larry Walker, to commercial tiers like Scott Sanchez or even dentist Dr. John Barr, I have discovered fascinating new techniques, tools and patterns. Every tier was encouraged to tie patterns with their own favorite tools and materials. In this book you will see several different vises from the traditional Thompson and Regal to the high tech rotary vise created by Andy Renzetti. Where possible, we have tried to photograph the tier wrapping their own flies (for example, the Mohawk fly where Heather LaFontaine's nail polish adds a note of authenticity as well as elegance).

Following the publication of *Volume II* of the *Jack Dennis Western Trout Fly Tying Manual* in 1980, I have often been asked why I did not publish another book soon after. The answer is simple. I needed the last dozen years or so to gather the patterns and techniques that I felt merited sharing with the fly tying community. Like a fine wine, it's time is now. From these talented fly tiers I have learned exciting new twists on old patterns, some fascinating new techniques, and even discovered some valuable new tools. The approach to tying these flies range from the classic methods of Chuck Stranahan and Mike Lawson to the avant garde antics of Gary LaFontaine.

I believe fly fishing and fly tying is an experience worth sharing. It is the reason for bringing together the tiers and their art in this book. Learning a new pattern, technique or fishing method should not be something you gain by means as surreptitious as industrial espionage. I have tried to create a book that simplifies the fly tier's art and craft rather than complicates the process. From the spiral binding to the exacting photos we believe we have created a manual that is comprehensive yet "user friendly". I know you will enjoy learning the new techniques and patterns and hope they will inspire you to innovate and experiment: push the fly tying envelope as my fly fishing friend Chuck Yeager might say.

There is a very basic premise to this book and the diverse group of fly tiers represented here share this premise when tying flies. They all tie flies with three things in mind. This triad is the underlying theme to this book. If you are enthusiastic about Norman McLean's "Fly fishing as religion" premise then this triad is my "Three Commandments".

The First Commandment: Thou shalt tie flies that are durable.

You are not catching fish if you spend all your time replacing a tattered fly. The materials and techniques presented here have evolved from the desire to create patterns that are tough enough to catch fish after fish.

The Second Commandment: Thou shalt tie flies that are easy and quick.

I used to tie thousands of flies every winter. It was how I made my living. Now with other business matters to tend to I'm lucky to tie a few dozen, and those are usually tied the evening before a fishing trip. I can sympathize with the guides who spend all day on the river and are then expected to tie up a fly box full of the next day's hot patterns. Necessity is the mother of invention and the guides have perfected the art of *NOT* complicating patterns.

The Third Commandment: Thou shalt tie flies that catch fish.

You would think this is obvious but a lot of fly patterns have been created to catch fishermen, not fish. As unusual as some of the names or appearances of some of the flies in this book may seem to you, I will guarantee each one has a winning track record. This doesn't mean each fly pattern will produce fish anytime and anywhere. While many of the patterns are effective almost anywhere, other patterns are more specific to a hatch or location. In this book, we've presented a broad spectrum of fly patterns and tying techniques. I know you will be able to fish many of these patterns with confidence on your home waters.

Most of us learned to fish our home waters through trial and error. This experience led to the formulation of a fly fishing logic we apply to fishing situations everywhere. From our earliest angling adventures we learned fish eat worms. Through further observation we discovered they would also eat bugs. As we became full fledged fly fishermen we discovered the "hatch". The "hatch", we learned, really involves a complete metamorphic cycle from nymph through emergers through dun and finally the

PREFACE

spent egg-laying adult. We also learned the trout is an extremely opportunistic feeder. Minnows, scuds, leeches, terrestrial insects or anything else that looks like a meal can be part of a trout's diet. This fishing logic applies to fly tying and, consequently, this is the way we have chosen to present the various patterns in this book. This book is divided into 6 sections: 1. Nymphs; 2. Emergers, Cripples, Stillborns; 3. Aquatic Adults; 4. Egg Laying Adults; 5. Terrestrials and Other Trout Food; 6. Attractors.

These sections fit our fishing logic well. However, they don't always fit the logic of a fish. Often a certain nymph pattern can be effectively used when fish are taking emergers, or an emerger pattern can be used for an adult, etc. As a fly fisherman, I enthusiastically look at these "crossover" flies as a great advantage when trying to determine the precise stage of a hatch.

I wish I could take all the credit for this book but I can't. I have to give inspirational credit to my Traveling Fly Fishing partners, Gary LaFontaine and Mike Lawson, who generously gave encouragement, advice, and time. Bruce James, editor of my *"Western Fly Tying Manual Volume II"*, again contributed a great deal of editorial expertise and deserves my heartfelt gratitude.

A book like this requires an enormous amount of coordination and research. My fly fishing and fly tying friend Joe Burke should get the lion's share of the credit for making this book happen. Without his tireless efforts and numerous trips around the West this book could not have been published.

Of course, the most important contributions come from the fly tiers themselves. Thanks, to all of you who have spent your lives creating and testing new patterns, most often without the recognition you deserve. I'm proud to be able to give credit where it is certainly due and I thank you for the fly tying knowledge I have gained. It's been fun, which after all, is the essence of fly tying, fly fishing and life itself.

ACKNOWLEDGMENTS

TOOLS & MATERIALS
Andy Renzetti - Renzetti Vise Co.
Ken Ligas - Scintilla Dubbing
Hugh Spencer - Spencer Hackles
Bernard Griffin - Griffin Enterprises
Ken Menard - Umpqua Feather Merchants
Larry Walker - Dubbit Tools
John Bailey - River Run Imports & Dai-Riki Hooks

TYPING
Stacey Caesar

COMPUTER INPUT
Bruce James

DESIGN
Rita Veisbergs
Jeanine Cappuccino
MediaWorks, Inc.
Jackson, Wyoming

ILLUSTRATIONS
Mike Stidham
Jeff Currier

SNAKE RIVER BOOK CO.
Brenda, George, Lorraine
Jackson, Wyoming

PRINTER
Blaine Hall
Sun Litho
Salt Lake City, Utah

EDITORIAL ASSISTANCE
Don Roberts
Bruce James

PHOTOGRAPHY
Mark Rohde - Front Cover & Instructional Photos
Don Roberts - Back Cover

OTHER PHOTOGRAPHY
Tom Montgomery
Andy Anderson
Jeff Currier

FRIENDS

JOHN BARR

John is a dentist from Boulder, Colorado and avid fly tier. He fishes for a variety of species including trout, warmwater fish and saltwater big game. Observations from his varied fly fishing experiences have led to the creation of his patterns which are featured by Umpqua Feather Merchants. Above all, his philosophy of fly tying is that patterns should be deadly producers and simple to tie. This philosophy is one of the cornerstones of this book.

PAT BERRY

Pat is a native of Maryland who now resides in Jackson, Wyoming where he works in the fly fishing department at Jack Dennis Outdoor Shop. He graduated from Middlebury College in Vermont where he majored in art. While in college he learned to tie flies from Peter Burton, a commercial fly tier and fly tying instructor in Middlebury, Vermont. Pat now commercially ties and his flies are in great demand. His meticulous style reflects his background in art.

JAY BUCHNER

Jay is one of the top fly tyers in the sport today. From their residence in Jackson, Wyoming he and his wife Kathy tie flies for anglers from around the world. Both were featured in *The Second Fly Tyers Almanac* and can usually be found demonstrating their skills at the annual FFF Conclave. Jay is a former fly shop owner in Jackson Hole and is one of the area's most respected guides. Many Jackson Hole tiers are his former students. In all respects he is a true master of the art of fly tying.

JOE BURKE

Joe is a respiratory therapist by trade who has been a long time resident of Jackson Hole. He devotes all of his spare time to his addiction to fly tying and fly fishing either in the production of videos and this book or guiding and doing some commercial fly tying. Joe sold his first flies when he was twelve years old at Roy's Barber Shop in his native Rockford, Illinois.

JACK DENNIS

Creator of the best selling WESTERN TROUT FLY TYING MANUAL Volumes I and II, Jack has been innovating in fly fishing for over thirty years. His contributions include videos, seminars, books, new teaching methods and the famous Jackson Hole One Fly event. Jack advises fly fishing tackle companies and consults with companies on international fly fishing travel.

RALPH HEADRICK

Ralph traded his surfboard for a fly rod when he moved from his native southern California home to Jackson Hole many years ago. He used to make a living as a guide and commercial fly tier, but now makes South Fork Skiff fishing boats with his friend and partner Paul Bruun. His custom tied flies are considered collectables.

FRIENDS

EMMETT HEATH

Emmett is the comsummate fly fishing guide who was named "Guide of the Year 1992" by *Fly Rod and Reel Magazine*. When not rowing his yellow drift boat down Utah's Green River he can either be found in Salt Lake City at Western Rivers Fly Fisher, of which he is part owner, or giving his slide show program to fly fishing clubs around the country. He has taught countless tiers in the Salt Lake area, many of whom have become tying instructors themselves.

BRUCE JAMES

Bruce is a long time guide and resident in the Jackson Hole where he is a an accomplished fly tier and has taught fly tying classes for many years. For several years he wrote a fishing column in the *Jackson Hole Guide* for which he won an award from the Wyoming Press Asssociation. This experience has allowed him to add considerable editorial expertise to this book as well as to *Jack Dennis' Western Trout Fly Tying Manual Volume II*.

JIMMY JONES

Jimmy owns and operates High Country Flies, a retail store and guide service in Jackson Hole. Like many other contributors to this book he is a guide, commercial fly tier, and fly tying instructor. Anyone who has ever fished with Jimmy knows him as an outstanding fly fisherman and a great reference on the area's fisheries.

FRIENDS

RANDALL KAUFMANN

Randall and his brother Lance own and operate Kaufmann's Streamborn fly fishing shops in Tigard, Oregon and in Bellevue and Seattle, Washington, as well as having one of the finest fly fishing catalog businesses around. He has authored *American Nymph Fly Tying Manual, Fly Tyers Nymph Manual, Tying Dry Flies, Bonefishing With A Fly* and co-authored *Lake Fishing With A Fly* with Ron Cordes. Randall has literally fly fished the world and is truly an expert source for fly tying and fly fishing information.

GARY LaFONTAINE

Author of *Caddisflies, Challenge Of The Trout, The Dry Fly-New Angles* and creator of the *River Rap audio tapes, Gary is an* innovative fly tier with many of his patterns featured by Umpqua Feather Merchants. He is also a media consultant and lecturer on fly tying and fishing. His writings hit the core of our fishing psyche while he entertains us with humor and his spirited nature. Gary has been involved in brainstorming of this new book as well as contributing a number of his innovative patterns for it. Gary lives in Deer Lodge, Montana with his family and fishing dog, Chester.

MIKE LAWSON

Considered one of the best fly fishing spring creek authorities, Mike lives on the banks of the Henry's Fork River in eastern Idaho. When not creating new patterns, Mike can be found operating Henry's Fork Anglers Fly Shop or casting to a finicky rainbow on the ranch. His reputation as a tier is well known as are his flies, many of which are featured by Umpqua Feather Merchants. Besides writing the forward to this book, Mike has helped in its formulation and has contributed many exciting patterns. An accomplished writer, program presenter and photographer, he has been a part of fly fishing videos and books, and has penned articles for almost all the fly fishing magazines. Mike is writing a book on spring creek fishing featuring the Henry's Fork and other spring creeks in the area.

FRIENDS

BEAR McKINNEY

Bear is a native of New Mexico who has fished and lived in Jackson Hole for many years. He is an outstanding fly fishing guide and instructor. Numerous area fly fishermen got their innitial instruction from "The Gentle Giant". Bear is also an expert fly tier who has spent hours learning techniques from the late Bing Lempke as well as other famous fly tiers. His fly tying classes are in great demand every winter in Jackson Hole.

SCOTT SANCHEZ

Scott works out of Jack Dennis Outdoor Shop in Jackson Hole as a guide, fly fishing and fly tying instructor, and general fly fishing guru who is a wealth of information on numerous freshwater and saltwater destinations. It's unlikely that there is anyone in fly tying who has used more nontraditional materials to create their innovative patterns than Scott. He has a nationwide clientelle of customers for his imaginative and durable flies.

CHUCK STRANAHAN

Chuck owns and operates Riverbend Flyfishing in Hamilton, Montana, in the heart of the Bitterroot Valley and is a regular on the winter show circuit in the West. His style is a perfect blend of innovation and classic fly tying technique which was learned from Cal Bird and other famous California masters. Many of his patterns are featured by Umpqua Feather Merchants. Chuck is a great source of information on Montana's Bitterroot River, a blue river fishery.

FRIENDS

DON STORMS

Don's business cards are inscribed "Artistic Flies..." and his patterns are truly works of art. His skills as a fly tier have earned him numerous awards on the east coast and his patterns have appeared in *American Angler* magazine. From his home in Oakridge, New Jersey, he shares his skills by teaching fly tying classes.

GUY TURCK

Guy is an accomplished guide, commercial fly tier and instructor who makes his home in Jackson Hole. When he is not on the river with a client, he is at his vise either experimenting with new patterns or tying, his famous Turck Tarantula, probably the most in-demand fly in the Jackson area. Guy is a quiet man with a gentle smile who really loves this sport and is a credit to it.

LARRY WALKER

Larry is a native of Rifle, Colorado, who started tying at twelve years old when his grandfather gave him tools and materials with the stipulation that he tie flies for he and his uncle Ted. He moved to Denver and went to work for the phone company in the early 60's and started tying flies for Jim and Jane Poor's Mountain View Tackle Shop. After retirement, he and his wife Sam opened up Walker's Fishin Hole in Lakewood, Colorado. After seven years they sold the business to devote all their time to his invention, the Dubbit. Larry can be found at many of the sport shows around the country. Don't miss him!

FRIENDS

GARY WILLMOTT
In all senses of the term, Gary is a true trout bum who has lived and fished in the mountain west for several years. He began tying flies to meet the demands of the fly fishing and guiding he does in Montana and Wyoming. Gary exhibits the typical philosophy of most fishing guides, maintaining that a pattern should be simple to tie, durable and catch fish.

TO MY FLY TYING FRIENDS

Because we share a special passion for angling with a fly, the experience
from our favorite sport has enriched our lives and has
probably taught us more about living than any other phase of our existence.
As fly tiers, we create an artificial from hair and feathers,
imitating God's own handiwork, to deceive a worthy adversary.
Fly tying is truly art, and among artists exists
a special creative and shared bond that lasts a lifetime.
This book is dedicated to that spirit.

JACK DENNIS

BASICS ON ESSENTIAL MATERIALS

HACKLES

When you go to purchase necks (also called capes) and saddles for hackling material, you will immediately realize where the biggest expense in fly tying is. If you know what to look for, your money can be well spent.

Hugh Spencer of Spencer Hackles in Plains, Montana, has the most accurate and concise guide for choosing hackles that I have seen. Hugh has been kind enough to allow us to quote him:

"The cape should have a glossy sheen. The higher the gloss, the more natural and alive your flies will look on the water.

"Choose a cape with a large range of feather sizes. This lets you tie more sizes of flies. But make sure the cape is heaviest in the sizes you use most. A cape with lots of 24's is great for a spring creek tier but of little use if you mainly fish #12 Wulff's.

"Be sure the cape has a good feather count. More feathers mean more flies; more flies mean more fish.

"Check for missing or damaged feathers. A quality cape will have all its feathers and very few, if any, tips will be broken. Birds occasionally do not feather-out completely and feathers can be easily broken. While still usable, broken feathers simply provide less length to tie.

"Feathers should be long with very little webbing. Webbing is the dense section at the lower end of the feather. Because it absorbs water, webbing will cause dry flies to sink. Length is desirable because a single long feather is often enough to tie a heavily hackled fly.

"Unlike the stem, the barbules should be stiff and extremely dense. Stiff barbs provide better support for your fly on the water. Likewise, the more barbules in contact with the water, the better the fly floats. The best hackles come from birds that have been genetically selected for stiff barbs, such as Spencer's.

"The stem should be supple. This is very important. Perhaps more dry fly problems arise from thick or stiff stems than from any other cause. Heavy stems are more likely to crack or break when the hackle is wrapped on the fly. In addition, the greater the diameter of the stem, the more oval it becomes, causing the feather to twist or roll rather than stand up when wrapped onto the hook.

"The barbules should be uniform in length along the entire portion of the stem above the webbing. This can be observed by bending the feather to separate the individual barbs. (Note: barbs located near the base among the webbing will be longer; the shorter this section is, the better, since it will be discarded.)"

THREADS

If all the flies we tied and fished were the same, then there would not be a need for different sizes and styles of hooks or thread. Fly tying and fly fishing wouldn't be much fun either. The fact of the matter is that there are thousands of fly patterns out there. They come in all sizes, styles and colors. Choosing the correct thread to tie a durable, well-proportioned fly is as essential as selecting the right hook.

Thread size starts with A-monocord and gets smaller. From there the next size down is 000 (3/0), with 000000 (6/0) being smaller than 3/0 and so on. Most fly tying thread in use today is nylon, but a few tiers stick to tradition and use silk thread. Waxed, rather than unwaxed thread is most commonly used today. It has been argued that waxed thread does not absorb head cement as well as unwaxed thread, and therefore the finished fly's durability may be in question. If you use a very thin head cement then this is a moot point. Tradition has also held that dry flies should be tied using waxed thread so as not to absorb water and sink, and that nymphs be tied with unwaxed thread to absorb water and sink. There comes a point where tradition must be weighted against practicality.

Here is a listing of different thread sizes with some suggestions for their use. As a simple rule of thumb, use the size which will give you the greatest number of thread wraps without distorting the proportions of the fly. More thread wraps equates to greater durability.

20/0 (Spider Web)	A very fine thread for use on the tiniest flies. Only available in white, which can be colored with a magic marker. It is fragile.
8/0	This thread is remarkably strong for its small diameter. It is excellent for small dry flies and nymphs sizes 14 through 24.
6/0	6/0 is an extremely versatile thread. It is excellent on dry flies sizes 4 through 14, and many nymphs, especially sizes 14 and 16. You may also use it to tie size 14 and 16 hairwing dry flies. It does have an application in tying certain small saltwater patterns.
3/0 (Monocord)	This is a strong medium diameter thread used on large dry flies especially hairwings, nymphs sizes 2 through 12, streamers and many saltwater patterns. It is a common choice of thread for spinning hair on small flies. It is to larger flies what 8/0 is to smaller flies.
A-Monocord	Its application to trout flies is common in tying streamers and leeches. Most tiers prefer it for spinning hair on flies such as hoppers and muddlers. It is strong. Larger, stronger thread makes it easier to flare and compress hair and bulky material.
Flat Waxed Nylon	Flat waxed nylon is versatile for larger dry and wet flies. It comes in a wide range of colors, which are useful to build underbodies and heads on large dry flies, streamers and saltwater patterns. It is strong, and possibly doesn't get enough attention from tiers.

HOOKS

Over the years, the number of companies manufacturing fly tying hooks has dramatically increased. The upside to this increased competition is that the variety of hook styles and quality has improved. Today's fly tying hooks are generally lighter, stronger and sharper than what was previously available.

The downside of having more hook manufacturers is the compounding of an old problem, lack of standardization of wire diameter, shank length and hook gape. All can vary significantly from one company's product to another's. One company's size 16 standard dry fly hook may be closer to another's size 14. This can be confusing and frustrating to many fly tiers.

The comparative chart that follows is simplified. It does not include all brands or styles of hooks, but rather those which are more routinely available. It is intended to help you select hooks to tie the flies in this book as well as most other trout flies. If you feel adventurous and want to experiment with different hooks, by all means do so. What's important is that your hook choice meets your fly tying and fishing demands.

If you want to learn about the history of hooks and their nomenclature, I recommend a modestly priced book by Dick Stewart, *The Hook Book*. Dick Talleur's, *The Versatile Fly Tyer*, and Darrel Martin's, *Fly Tying Methods* are also excellent sources of reference on hooks.

Lastly, I highly recommend the use of barbless hooks, or hooks with the barbs pinched down. This can greatly reduce the trauma of handling your catch, which will in turn increase the fish's chance of survival when you release it. Also, I don't know a single fisherman or fishing guide who has not had a hook penetrate their clothing or flesh. A barbless or debarbed hook is always easier and more painless to remove than a barbed one.

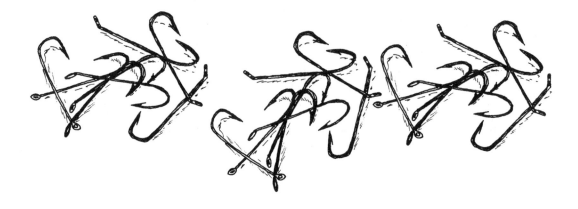

HOOK CHART

Surface Flies	Dai-Riki	Mustad	Tiemco	Daiichi	Additional Hooks
Standard Dry Fly Hook, Downeye	305	94840 AC 94840 AC 80000 BR	TMC 100 TMC 921 TMC 5210	1310 1170 1180	
Barbless Dry Fly Hook	None	94845	TMC 900 BL	1190	
Straight Eye Dry Fly Hook	310	94859	TMC 101 TMC 501	1480 1640	
Up-eye Dry Fly Hooks	None	94842	TMC 500 ll	1330	
Fine Wire Dry Fly	300	94833 AC 94833	TMC 5290	1480 (Straight Eye)	
Fine Wire 2x-3x Long Dry Fly Hook	None	94831	TMC 2312 TMC 2302 TMC 5212	None	

Subsurface Flies	Dai-Riki	Mustad	Tiemco	Daiichi	Additional Hooks
Standard Sproat	070 075 (heavy wire)	3906 AC 3906	TMC 3769	1530 (1x short) 1550	
1x Long	070	3906 B AC 3906 B 7957 B	TMC 3761	1560	
2x Long	730	9671 AC 9671	TMC 5262	1710	
3x Long	710 270 (curved)	9672 AC 9672 AC 80050 BR (curved)	TMC 5263 TMC 200R (curved)	2461 1720 1270 (curved)	
4x Long	700 700B (bent shank)	9674 79580 AC 79580	TMC 9394 TMC 9395	2220 1750	
6x Long	None	9575 36620 AC 36890	TMC 300	2340 J171	
Scud, Caddis Pupa Hook	135	AC 80250 BR AC 80200 BR	TMC 2457 TMC 2487	1130 1150 J220	

NYMPHS

CRANEFLY LARVA

Jack Dennis

There are a number of species of cranefly larva distributed throughout North America. They are found in both aquatic and semi-aquatic habitats. One group of cranefly larva, the genus Tipula can offer an opportunistic food source for trout. Ernest Schwiebert's book, *Nymphs*, is a good basic reference for cranefly larva and other aquatic trout food you might be trying to imitate at your vise.

My good friend, Emmett Heath, the dean of guides on Utah's Green River, made this statement: "This large nymph has accounted for more giant fish caught on the Green than any other pattern. The cranefly larva lives in the moss and under stones along the bottom. Generally, it must be fished bouncing the bottom."

The Cranefly Larva is not a difficult fly to tie. Start by heavily weighting the hook shank. These wormlike bugs inhabit the dead material and mud on the bottom of lakes and streams, not the surface film. There are times when you can actually see trout rutting around with their noses in the mud looking for cranefly larva. You may need to put additional lead on the leader or even use a full sinking line to get this fly down.

Size is another key when tying this fly, especially the Giant Cranefly Larva. The larva elongates and contracts it's body for locomotion, so the trout see naturals in sizes big and bigger. In tailwater fisheries, such as Utah's Green River, the sudden release of large volumes of water to meet electrical demands can dislodge cranefly larva from the stream bottom. These dislodged naturals will curl their bodies for protection, so you may want to curve the hook shank with a pair of pliers to mimic this shape.

Other considerations when tying this fly are body color and translucence. Common colors are gray and olive, but pale cream, tan and dirty orange are locally common. When choosing a dubbing material for this and many other nymph patterns, keep in mind that the body should give the illusion of transparency. Antron or Angora goat dubbing will do the trick. The Dubbit dubbing loop tool and the Renzetti rotary vise are ideal for efficiently tying this pattern.

CRANEFLY LARVA

HOOK:	Dai-Riki 700 or equivalent, sizes 2-8
THREAD:	3/0 olive monocord or contrasting color
LEAD:	.030 - .035
TAIL:	Clump of fibers from pheasant tail feather
BODY:	Olive Angora goat or color of natural
RIBBING:	Med. copper or gold wire
HEAD:	Tan or dun Angora goat or color of natural

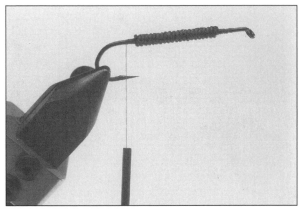

1. Heavily lead the hook shank as shown.

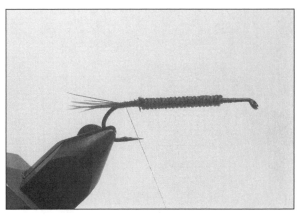

2. Secure clump of fibers from a pheasant tail feather.

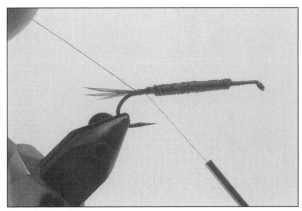

3. Tie in the wire ribbing.

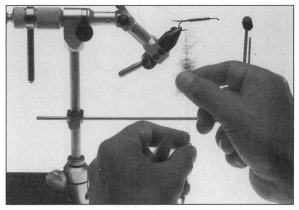

4. After forming a dubbing loop with the Dubbit and closing the loop with a few turns, jam the goat dubbing into the loop as shown.

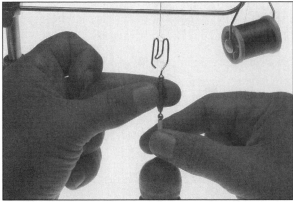

5. Spin the Dubbit tool, just like snapping the fingers of your left hand. You should not use downward pressure to tighten the loop.

6. Dubbed loop ready to wrap forward to form the body.

7. Rib the body.

8. Dub a light colored head with the same dubbing loop technique.

9. Pick out the dubbing with a bodkin or teaser to give a translucence to the fly when it is wet.

10. Finished Cranefly Larva. At this point the hook can be bent with pliers if you want a curved body.

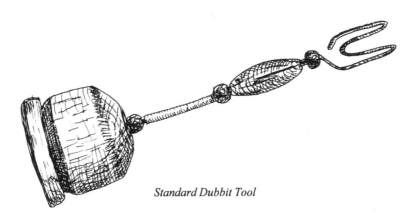

Standard Dubbit Tool

FURIMSKY'S NYMPH

Larry Walker

A gentleman by the name of Chuck Furimsky invited me to tie flies at the fishing shows he promotes in Pennsylvania and New Jersey. It was a chance for me to meet some other fly tiers and fishermen, as well as demonstrate some unique fly tying techniques with my Dubbit tool.

First, I did the loop technique, which creates a tighter dubbed body than single strand dubbing. Next, I did cross-cut dubbing to achieve a translucent body. Gary LaFontaine has tremendous success with translucence on his sparkle yarn flies using a similar method. Finally, I looped a soft hackle to give the delicate soft feathers more strength and loft.

I just happened to demonstrate all three techniques on the same hook. I glanced at it, then looked up at the people watching me. I saw lights going on and heard bells ringing in their minds. They were saying, "I can't wait to get back to my bench." Obviously, there was a lot of interest in the fly. The soft hackle demonstration fly was passed around. There were plenty of suggestions about color combinations and the use of various kinds of soft hackle feathers.

I wandered around that eastern show with my "accident fly" showing it to other tiers, getting their opinions, and trying to think of a name. As I wandered, it occurred to me that Chuck Furimsky had taken a big gamble putting this fly fishing only show together. Chuck worked hard and worried. His program was a big success. It will have a positive impact on the sport of fly fishing and will help all of us in the business. So, with a little smile and a lot of appreciation, Furimsky's Nymph it is.

Soft hackle flies are certainly not new. What I have attempted to do is to modify the traditional approach to soft hackles of always sparse or always partridge feathers. A soft hackle nymph does not necessarily have to be sparse. I prefer a somewhat full appearance to my soft hackle flies.

The cross-cut dubbing technique used on the thorax of this soft hackle nymph is very effective on other patterns. It caused me to change my woven stonefly pattern. The fly has a more lifelike appearance and it fishes significantly better. Instead of a loop dubbed fur thorax, I now cross-cut dub it. I used to pre-cut dubbing fibers to a desired length before inserting them into the cross-cut loop. Joe Burke of Snake River Book Company told me he found it easier to put material in the loop first, then cut it to size. He's right, especially on hooks larger than size 16.

The Furimsky's Nymph and its variations can be tied without having an anxiety attack. Most of all, they will catch fish.

FURIMSKY'S NYMPH

HOOK: Dai-Riki 070, Tiemco 3769 or equivalent, sizes 8-16
THREAD: 8/0 black or color to contrast
ABDOMEN: Orange goose biot or color of choice
THORAX: Olive Scintilla dubbing or color to contrast with abdomen
HACKLE: Soft mottled brown hen, partridge or grouse body
feather

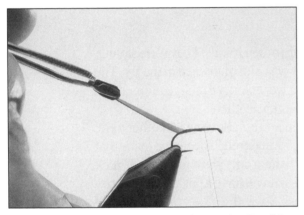

1. Secure the butt of a goose biot on the far side of the hook.

2. Wrap the goose biot forward to the rear of the thorax and tie off.

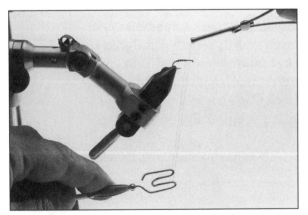

3. Form a dubbing loop with the Dubbit tool.

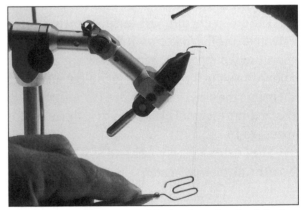

4. Come over the top with the thread to lock in the loop.

5. Insert a thin layer of dubbing material into the loop as shown.

6. Trim both the right and left sides of the dubbing to form a single strip of material in the loop.

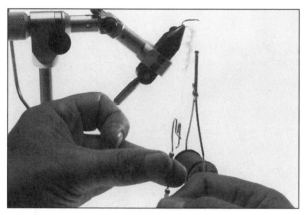

7. Spin the Dubbit tool as shown.

8. Spun loop of cross-cut dubbing ready to be wrapped.

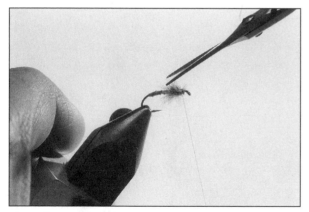

9. After wrapping thorax trim it to shape.

10. Tie in the butt of a grouse feather to the far side of the hook leaving a little of the bare stem exposed. This makes it wrap easier.

11. Using hackle pliers make 6 to 8 turns of the feather around the thread.

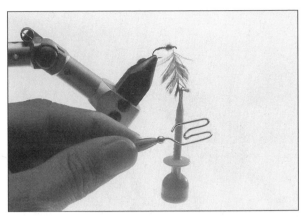

12. Form another dubbing loop with the Dubbit as shown.

13. Close off the top of the loop by bringing the thread over the top from right to left and securing the thread around the hook.

14. Spin the Dubbit only a few turns to create the spun feather as shown.

15. Make 2 to 4 turns of hackle pulling back the fibers of the previous turns with your fingers. Whip finish.

16. Finished Furimsky's Nymph.

CAREY SPECIAL

Jay Buchner

When I first came to Jackson Hole in 1968, I eagerly prospected the local fishing tackle emporiums for fly suggestions. One fly that was frequently pointed out was a bright wet fly, the Carey Special. They were simply tied chenille bodies of bright orange, chartreuse or yellow, and a pheasant rump feather for the tail and hackle. Today you can't find one in any of the fly shops.

The Carey Special was originated in the Northwest about 1925 by Dr. Day and Col. Carey. The original was thought to have been tied with a brown bear hair tail and body. I prefer to tie and fish it using this traditional material. It's origin was as a lake pattern, but I find it to be just as effective in rivers.

Even though it has fallen from popularity in fly shops, the trout don't know it. The Carey Special continues to be very successful for me as a general imitation of a dragonfly, caddis, damselfly or dobsonfly larva.

CAREY SPECIAL

HOOK:	Mustad 3906B or equivalent, sizes 8-14
THREAD:	3/0 black monocord
TAIL:	Black or brown bear hair
BODY:	Black or brown bear hair
HACKLE:	Pheasant rump feather

1. After wrapping rear 2/3 of hook shank with thread attach several strands of bear hair for tail as shown.

2. Tie in several more strands of bear hair as shown.

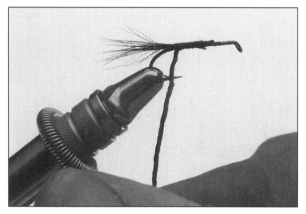

3. Twist hair to form a rope.

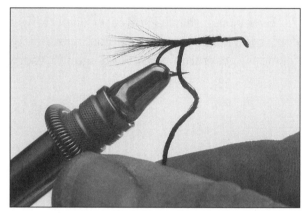

4. Finished hair rope.

5. Wrap the rope forward to form a segmented body.

6. Select a pheasant rump feather to be used for the hackle.

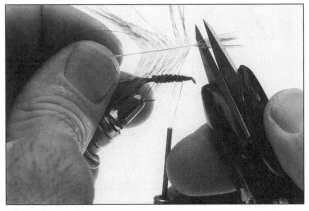

7. Strip the fibers from the base of the feather; stroke the fibers back towards the butt and trim the tip as shown.

8. Head on view of the fly in the vise. Fold the fibers from the right and left side of the stem to one side. Tie in with tip of feather facing forward.

9. Side view of hackle ready to be wrapped.

10. Wrap hackle forward 2 to 4 turns pulling back fibers before each new wrap. Whip finish the head.

11. Finished Carey Special.

BLACK MARTINEZ NYMPH

Jack Dennis

Don Martinez started tying flies in the 1930's. He loved the Rocky Mountains and spent every summer fishing and touring in the region. His flies began appearing in the better tackle shops during the 1940's. One of his friends was the legendary Dan Bailey of Livingston, Montana. Dan believed that Don was the father of the modern Woolly Worm. In his book, *Montana Trout Flies*, George Grant mentions Don's contribution of a thick chenille body to the Woolly Worm and goes on to say, "Martinez used to tie them without a vise when he talked to and waited on customers in his West Yellowstone shop."

Don loved to collaborate on fly patterns with guides and well known fishermen of the West. One of his best known flies was called the Whitcraft. His friend, the late Bob Carmichael of Moose, Wyoming, helped design the fly to match the Black Quill hatch that was so common in the early season.

Roy Donnelly, a steelhead fly tier from San Diego, California had a great influence on Don. The two became lifelong friends and shared many fly tying methods. Don taught Roy the gentle art of tying dry flies, while Roy taught Don his methods of tying soft hackles. Roy probably knew more about wet flies than any man alive during the 1940's and 1950's. Eventually, both Don and Roy could tie dry flies, in the words of Bob Carmichael, "...so lifelike you expect them to fly out of your hand...delicately dressed and perfectly balanced..."

While both received accolades for their dry fly patterns, they loved the art of tying and fishing wet flies. They believed that the secret of fishing flies below the surface was to tie the pattern with a soft hackle. It gave the fly movement and the impression of a live insect. In the winter they would travel to Mexico to search out the losers of the cock fights that might have just the right hackle. After the trip, they would return home to wrap their season's supply of flies.

Eventually, Don spent his summers in West Yellowstone, Montana and opened a small tackle shop in the garage of his home there. It marked the beginning of West Yellowstone fly shops. Bud Lilly and Jim Danskin soon followed in Don's footsteps.

During his time in West Yellowstone, Don became interested in tying and fishing nymphs. He experimented with a variety of materials and invented the Martinez series of flies to imitate mayfly nymphs. By using different colors of raffia (African grass) for the wingcase, he could create different looks in his nymphs. His friend Roy Donnelly suggested a guinea feather for a soft hackle. This has become an essential part of the Martinez Nymph.

While body colors ranging from brown to dun can be used, it is black which has the greatest popularity. The Black Martinez Nymph is an effective imitation of mayfly and stonefly nymphs in most Yellowstone area rivers.

Don Martinez was truly one of the great early Western fly tiers. The fly which bears his name, the Black Martinez Nymph is a pattern you should tie and fish. You will be pleasantly surprised with the results.

BLACK MARTINEZ

HOOK:	Dai-Riki 730 or equivalent, sizes 8-14
THREAD:	6/0 black
LEAD:	.020 - .025
TAIL:	Guinea feather
BODY:	Black angora goat
RIBBING:	Fine oval tinsel, silver or gold
THORAX:	Black angora goat
WINGCASE:	Green raffia
HACKLE:	Guinea feather to size

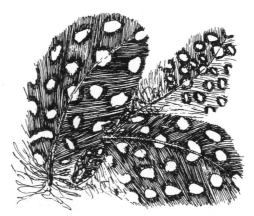

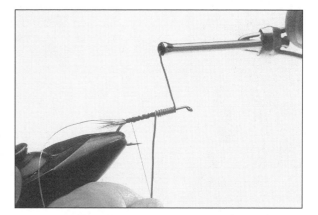

1. Starting about halfway down the shank tie in a small bunch of fibers from a Guinea hen feather. The fibers should extend a hook gape past the bend of the hook.

2. Attach the fine oval rib at the same halfway thread point. Then wrap lead around the front half of the hook as shown.

3. Put a dubbing loop in the thread and make a couple of turns; this will allow the dubbing to be jammed in and stay put.

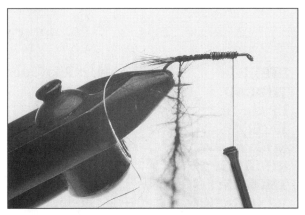

4. Once the dubbing is in the loop, spin the dubbing tool which locks the dubbing in place and makes a fuzzy chenille.

5. Wrap a tapered abdomen as shown.

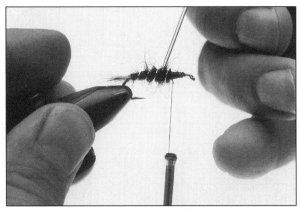

6. Rib the abdomen with fine oval and secure with thread. With a bodkin pick out some of the Angora goat dubbing to create a buggy look.

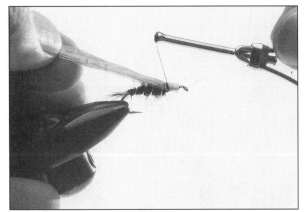

7. Attach green raffia wing case material as shown.

8. Make another dubbing loop of the same material used for the abdomen.

9. After spinning the loop wind a thorax with the taper as shown.

10. After pulling the raffia forward and securing with thread to form a wing case, tie in a single Guinea feather to the top of the hook as shown.

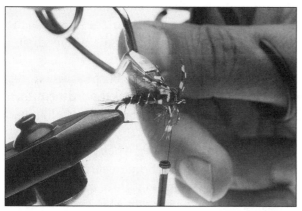

11. Using hackle pliers, make 2 or 3 turns of the Guinea feather. Note the length of the fibers in proportion to the size of the fly.

12. Finished Black Martinez Nymph after whip finishing and gluing the head.

SERENDIPITY

Joe Burke

While many different people take credit for originating the Serendipity, no one seems to know where the name came from. It is fair to say that the Serendipity was developed as a Madison River pattern, probably in the last ten or so years. It's popularity has skyrocketed in the past three or four years.

Mike Lawson of the Henry's Fork Anglers in Last Chance, Idaho recounts the first time he saw it:

"I thought it looked ridiculous, but it worked. The fly as I know it was developed by Dom Traverso, who teaches high school and coaches baseball in Dixon, California and guides for our shop in the summer. Dom ties it differently than the Serendipities I see in other shops. He puts weight on the rear of the fly so that the tail hangs down while the head is upright. In fact, my guides and I didn't call it a Serendipity; we called it Dom's fly.

"Dom was having some spectacular success with some not too accomplished clients using his fly pattern. He would have them fish it straight upstream, let it drift back toward them, then lift and strip the line. He would tell them to set the hook if they felt resistance because they had a fish.

"Dom wanted to keep a good thing under wraps, so he objected when I first wanted to feature it in the shop. I still don't think it is like the Serendipity. Somewhere in my mind I remember that the late Ross Merigold had something to do with the origin of the Serendipity. It is interesting that both Dom and Ross were using these patterns on the Madison at the same time."

John Juracek who, along with Craig Mathews, owns and operates Blue Ribbon Flies in West Yellowstone, Montana (and co-authored an outstanding book with Craig, *Fly Patterns of Yellowstone*) remembers that Ross Merigold first showed him the Serendipity. John said:

"Ross used it as a midge larva and fished it dead drift on the bottom. At the time, not many anglers recognized the significance of midge larva on the Madison. People were pretty much using Pheasant Tails as a mayfly imitation, or something like Ross' R.A.M. Caddis to imitate caddis larva or emerging caddis pupa. The Serendipity not only imitates a midge larva, but easily crosses over to imitate mayfly and free living caddis nymphs.

"Lance Vines was the first of our guides to use it. About 5 years ago he had some clients who had fished before with Ross. They showed some of Ross' flies to Lance who said not to use them because they wouldn't catch anything. They used them anyway and to Lance's amazement, caught a lot of fish. Well, you just can't keep success of that magnitude a secret for long. Pretty soon all of our guides were using it. Even the most novice fly fishermen were catching big numbers of fish. It is hard to explain it's success, but it easily outfished the Pheasant Tail Nymphs by ten to one.

"The colors that seem to work best are brown, olive and red, but gray and chartreuse can be good. We carry them in sizes 14 through 22. Overall, size 16 is best but size 22 works well in the surface film.

"You know, a lot of people look at the deer hair head on the Serendipity and think it is meant to float the fly. Ross said that the guy who showed him a similar pattern had intended to use white hen hackle for the head, as Ross had done on his R.A.M. Caddis. When he sat down at his tying bench he found that he didn't have any white hen hackle so he used something that he did have a lot of, deer hair."

The *American Heritage Dictionary* defines serendipity as, "The faculty of making valuable discoveries by accident." The origin of the deer hair head on the Serendipity just might be the mysterious source of the pattern's name.

SERENDIPITY

HOOK: Tiemco 2487, DaiRiki 135 or equivalent, sizes 10-22
THREAD: 6/0 or 8/0 black or color to contrast
BODY: Z-lon, color to match natural midge or caddis larva
RIBBING: Fine gold wire or color to contrast with body color
HEAD: Pearl color Krystal Flash and deer hair(can substitute a bead head)

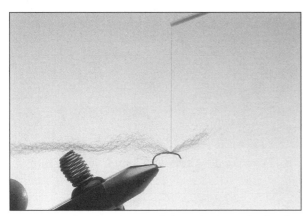

1. Make an underbody of thread along the hook shank then tie in the Z-lon as shown.

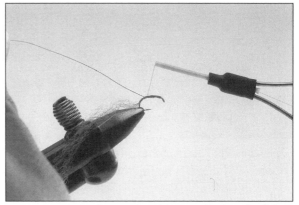

2. Wrap thread over the Z-lon to the bend of the hook then tie in fine wire gold ribbing to the top of the hook.

3. Twist the Z-lon to form a single ropelike strand and wrap the body forward to behind the eye leaving room for the head.

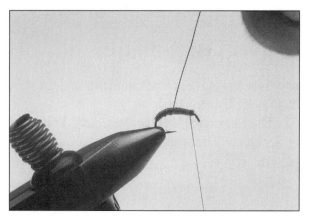

4. This is an optional way to form a body. Wrap the Z-lon forward without twisting and rib with the wire. Leave room for the head.

5. Attach 6 to 8 strands of pearl Krystal Flash as shown.

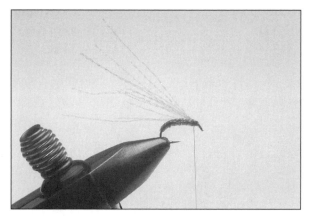

6. Pull the forward segment of Krystal Flash back and secure with thread wraps.

7. Place deer hair over the top of the Krystal Flash as shown. Length is not important.

8. Flare the deer hair with 2 or 3 wraps of thread.

9. Pull the forward ends of the hair back a few at a time and secure each time with a wrap of thread.

10. Fly shown whip finished and ready to be trimmed.

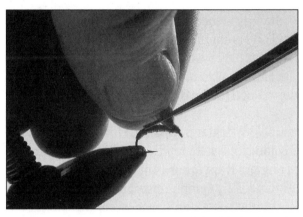

11. Grab the entire bulk of material with the thumb and index finger and cut to length all at once.

12. Finished Serendipity.

BULLER CADDIS

Jack Dennis

My numerous trips to New Zealand have given me the chance to meet many interesting people. One of these is Tony Entwhistle, with whom I have shared many exciting fishing experiences. He is one of the finest fly fishermen and fly tiers I have ever met.

Tony operates Rod & Gun Expeditions located in the Nelson Lake National Park region of the South Island. A passionate believer in wild trout and an articulate writer, Tony has found himself at the forefront of the New Zealand fishing scene. He was president of the New Zealand Guides Association and a stern advocate of protecting the streams of New Zealand. Even though catch and release is relatively new to New Zealand, Tony has pioneered the way in the Nelson area.

A day with Tony is unique and blessed with discovery and wonderment. It was he who exposed me to the two fly system and helped hone my skills at fishing deep with heavily weighted nymphs. He also introduced me to one of the best nymph patterns I have ever used, the Buller Caddis (named for the Buller River in the Nelson Lake district).

Caddis are an important food source in New Zealand streams. However, due to the crystalline clarity of the water, the fish get a good look at their prey and are not easily fooled by imitations. Because Tony has guided anglers from around the world, he has had the opportunity to fish an almost endless variety of caddisfly nymph imitations. By experimenting with different materials, he has found that Australian opossum is an ideal color and texture to use as a dubbing to imitate natural caddisfly nymphs. In Tony's opinion, weighting the nymph is also essential, because it must sink to the proper depth quickly.

The Buller Caddis will work anywhere in the world. I have had extremely good luck with this fly on the Henry's Fork, Madison, Big Hole and Green River. Australian opossum fur is available from many fly shops and mail order catalogs. Pick up some of this unique fur and tie the Buller Caddis. It might give you the edge in the next caddis water you encounter. As they say in New Zealand, "Give it a go."

BULLER CADDIS

HOOK:	Dai-Riki 710 or equivalent, sizes 8-16
THREAD:	6/0 black or brown
TAIL:	Black Australian opossum or black calf body hair
BODY:	Mixed guard hair & fur from Australian opossum
LEAD:	.020
RIBBING:	Fine copper wire
WINGCASE:	4 strands or peacock herl
HEAD:	Reddish color Australian opossum body fur, especially flank fur

1. Tie in a clump of black hair from Australian Opossum or black calf body hair as shown.

2. Secure fine copper wire to the top of the hook shank.

3. Lead the hook shank from above the barb to 1/3 back from the eye. Form a dubbing loop and lock with thread.

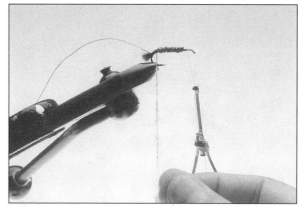

4. Turn the dubbing tool a few times closing the upper portion of the loop. This makes it easy to jam dubbing into position in the loop.

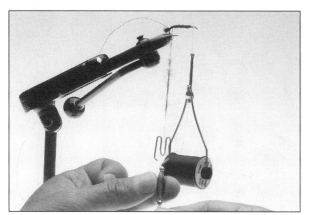

5. Spin the Dubbit forming a fuzzy yarn as shown.

6. Wrap an abdomen with the looped material starting around the bend of the hook; this angles the tail downward.

7. Rib through the abdomen with the copper wire.

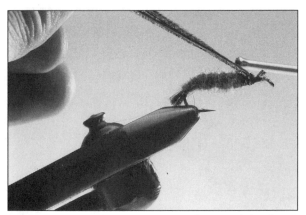

8. Tie in the tips of 4 strands of peacock herl.

9. Dub the head using a lighter contrasting color fur.

10. Notice the shape of body and head. Taper is only at the rear of the fly.

11. Pull the peacock herl strands over to form a wing case and tie down. Whip finish.

12. Finished Buller Caddis.

ALL ROUNDER MAYFLY NYMPH

John Barr

Let me start by making a few comments about my philosophies concerning fly patterns. First and most important, a pattern must have a good track record on a lot of different waters over a period of years. You can't just invent a good looking pattern, catch some fish on it, and say, "This is a great fly". I also feel that flies should be easy to tie, durable and use materials that are readily available.

I am a great believer in flies that are both realistic and impressionistic. The fly should look good, but still have a lot of moving parts. Many realistic patterns appeal to the eye, but they look like sticks in the water and take an hour to tie. I believe my patterns combine the best of both the realistic and impressionistic worlds, and their track record of catching fish through the years proves them out.

My nymphs are unweighed, since I prefer to sink them to a desired depth with split shot. The nymph has some weight from the hook and water soaked materials. There is also a neutral or balanced buoyancy to the unweighted nymph which allows it to naturally seek out the feeding lanes, rather than plummet to the bottom.

Natural nymphs are generally curled when free drifting. I feel more confident fishing a sunken nymph tied on a curved hook.

There is a lot of confusion about exact color and the number of patterns one should carry. After reading articles, books and catalogues, some fishermen figure they need to carry a thousand different patterns in one hundred different colors. My biggest problem in fishing is not which pattern, but finding good conditions (water, wind, etc.), finding a hatch and having fish on a good bite. If things are right, you just need a good basic selection of patterns in a variety of sizes and a few basic colors; with a proper presentation you will catch fish most of the time.

I carry a basic nucleus of patterns that I call All Rounders, which are going to work the majority of the time. I don't spend half the day changing patterns because if the fish are on a bite and I have an appropriate fly (you don't fish a dragonfly nymph during a midge hatch), one of my All Rounders is usually going to work.

The All Rounder Mayfly Nymph is easy to tie and very productive when it doesn't seem like much is going on. I have had countless enjoyable days on the stream with this generic pattern.

ALL ROUNDER MAYFLY NYMPH

HOOK:	Tiemco 2457, Dai-Riki 135 or equivalent, sizes 10-18
THREAD:	8/0 brown
TAIL:	Brown Hungarian partridge body feather fibers
BODY:	Brown/olive synthetic dubbing such as Scintilla
LEGS:	Brown Hungarian partridge body feather fibers
WINGCASE:	Brown Hungarian partridge feather fibers

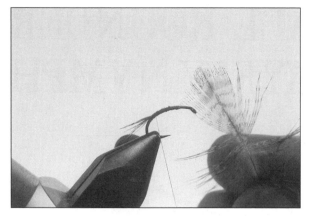

1. Tie in several fibers from a partridge body feather to form a tail.

2. Dub a body and wrap it forward in a taper to the thorax.

3. Tie in fibers from the partridge wing feather as shown.

4. Tie in several fibers from a partridge body feather with the tips pointing back no further than the hook point. Trim fiber butts.

5. After dubbing thorax pull the fibers from the wing feather (step 3) forward to form the wing case as shown. Whip finish.

6. The finished All Rounder Mayfly Nymph.

ALL ROUNDER DAMSEL NYMPH

John Barr

I would bet hard money that no other aquatic insect imitation brings more big fish to anglers' nets in stillwaters than a damselfly nymph does. Let's be honest, the largest, most muscular fish live in lakes. The biggest problem fishing lakes is locating the fish. A damselfly nymph can solve that problem. When natural damsel nymphs are swimming along the shoreline, trout, including some of the largest in the lake, come into the shallows to gorge on them, gulping and boiling to show their position.

I started fishing damselfly nymphs about 20 years ago on Idaho's Henry's Lake. Since that time, I have tied and fished many different patterns including wiggle tails. The All Rounder Damsel Nymph is the culmination of all those years of trial and error and has become my most effective pattern.

Most commercially tied damselfly nymphs are far too bulky in the rear. Naturals have a very slight abdomen. I have also noticed that fish don't seem to be finicky about the color of a damsel imitation, even though the color of naturals varies from pond to pond and often within the same pond. Brown/olive is the only color I tie and fish. Lastly, my All Rounder Damsel Nymph looks succulent when it is wet, while other patterns I have seen don't have that lifelike quality.

The All Rounder Damsel Nymph is an excellent warm water pattern because nearly every bass pond in America is full of damsels. Panfish will garbage the pattern and in still, clear water tough bass will suck it in with authority when something more garish might spook them.

There are a few bass ponds near my office where I like to spend my lunch breaks. Like all stillwater fisheries, they are loaded with damselfly and dragonfly nymphs. While I generally use an All Rounder Dragonfly Nymph when blind fishing if it is dead calm, I like to sight fish with the All Rounder Damselfly Nymph.

I recall one particularly large bass that I unsuccessfully fished to on a number of days. This big guy was stoic to the point of looking like a mounted fish until the day I cast a size 10 All Rounder Damsel Nymph in front of him. A picture of the smile on my face the moment that big bass inhaled my fly could hang in my dental office as an advertisement for healthy teeth. That big grin has been repeated by me and my fishing buddies countless times over the years when we have fished my pattern in both warm water bass ponds and cold water trout lakes.

ALL ROUNDER DAMSEL NYMPH

HOOK: Tiemco 9394, Mustad 9674 or equivalent, sizes 8-12
THREAD: 3/0 olive monocord
TAIL: Soft marabou like fibers at the base of an olive dyed   mallard flank feather or olive dyed marabou
BODY: Olive brown synthetic dubbing such as Scintilla
LEGS: Stiffer fibers from olive dyed mallard flank
EYES: Extra small Umpqua mono nymph eyes
BACK: Plastic cut from Ziploc bag
RIBBING: 4X mono

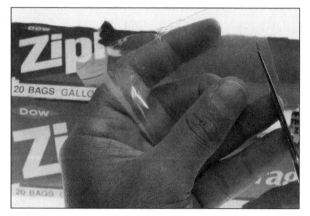

1. Tie in a tail of soft fibers from mallard flank feather as shown.

2. Tie in a piece of 4x mono to the far side of the hook shank. This will be the ribbing.

3. Cut a segment of Ziploc bag in a slight taper as shown. This will be the overbody.

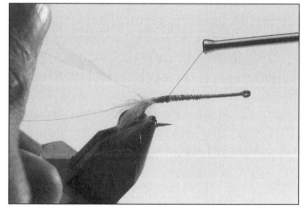

4. Tie in the small end of plastic at the rear of the hook.

5. Dub a slight body with a subtle taper forward.

6. Tie in stiffer fibers from a mallard flank feather to form legs on the right and left side of the fly.

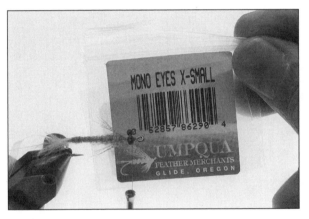

7. Tie on eyes.

8. Secure eyes by ' X-ing ' with the thread wraps.

9. Dub the thorax and head as shown. Make sure to ' X-wrap ' through the eyes.

10. Pull the plastic overbody forward and secure with several thread wraps.

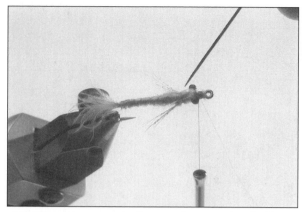

11. Rib the abdomen with the mono segmenting evenly.

12. Wrap the mono to form a wing case just in front of the legs and behind the eyes as shown; after one half turn of mono in front of the eyes tie off and whip finish.

13. The finished All Rounder Damsel Nymph.

ALL ROUNDER DRAGONFLY NYMPH

John Barr

Blind casting the All Rounder Dragonfly Nymph with my four weight fly rod on some local ponds is one of my favorite ways to spend a morning or evening. You never know what will rip it. I've landed bass to 6½ pounds, and my largest bluegill, pumpkinseed and crappie have fallen to this pattern. I've landed golden carp to 16 pounds using it. You hook tailers on the flats and they take off just like a redfish, which they look like. I have also hooked, but not landed, grass carp (they are missiles) in the 20 to 30 pound category using the All Rounder Dragonfly Nymph. It seems that all warm water fisheries on earth are full of dragonflies, so it is understandable that a fly tied to imitate the natural should work so well.

The All Rounder Dragonfly Nymph is not limited to warm water use. The largest trout I have caught from lakes have fallen to it. Needless to say, I fish it with confidence.

ALL ROUNDER DRAGONFLY NYMPH

HOOK:	Tiemco 5262, Dai-Riki 730 or equivalent, sizes 4-8
THREAD:	3/0 brown
TAIL:	Clump of black marabou
BODY:	Brown/olive synthetic dubbing such as Scintilla
LEGS:	Black hen hackle of poor grade
BACK:	Plastic cut from Ziploc bag
EYES:	Size small Umpqua mono nymph eyes
RIBBING:	3X mono

1. Tie in a clump of marabou fibers for a tail.

2. Secure 3x mono for ribbing and a cut Ziploc strip as in the All Rounder Damsel Nymph, page 50, step 3.

3. After dubbing a fat tapered abdomen tie in the butt of the hen hackle feather.

4. Secure the mono eyes just as in the All Rounder Damsel Nymph.

5. Dub the remaining thorax and 'X' through the eyes.

6. Use a dark felt tip pen to color the dubbing on the back of the fly.

7. Palmer hen hackle through thorax to form legs.

8. Pull the plastic strip forward and secure at the eye of the hook.

9. Rib with mono to segment and form wing case just as in the All Rounder Damselfly Nymph. Whip finish.

10. Make a small cut at the rear of the wing case to slightly flare it.

11. With a dubbing teaser or bodkin, pick out the body to give it a buggy appearance.

12. Side and top view of the All Rounder Dragonfly Nymph.

NET BUILDER

John Barr

Uncased caddis larva are prevalent in riffles and fast runs of trout streams across the U.S. Some of these uncased caddis larva build nets to attach themselves to rocks or debris, while others are free living. They are found in incredible densities in streams such as Montana's Madison River, and surely comprise a significant percentage of the trout's annual dietary intake. It is surprising that many fly fishermen overlook the significance of this nymph.

Although I call my pattern the Net Builder, it works equally well as a free living caddis. Green seems to be the most widespread color, but cream or amber colored uncased caddis larva are locally common. The Net Builder is also a good crossover imitation of an aquatic beetle, cranefly larva or even a scud.

NET BUILDER

HOOK:	Tiemco 2457, Dai-Riki 135 or equivalent, sizes 8-16
THREAD:	3/0 brown monocord
TAIL:	Gray ostrich herl
BODY:	Synthetic dubbing such as Scintilla, either green, cream or amber
BACK:	Plastic cut from Ziploc bag

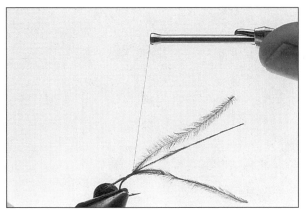

1. Tie in 3 or 4 strands of ostrich herl for a tail. These can be tips or trimmed broken pieces of herl.

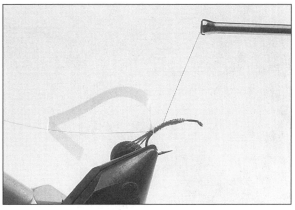

2. Tie in mono ribbing and cut Ziploc plastic as shown.

3. Dub a tapered abdomen to the point shown.

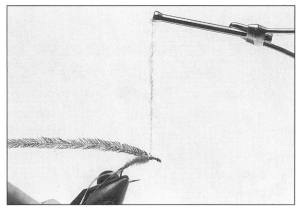

4. Tie in another ostrich herl and dub a thorax.

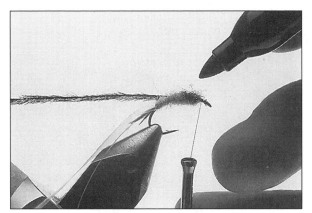

5. Darken the dubbed thorax with a felt tip pen.

6. Wrap the ostrich herl through the thorax.

7. Pull the plastic strip forward and secure as shown.

8. Rib to the head with the mono forming progressively larger segments especially through the thorax. Whip finish.

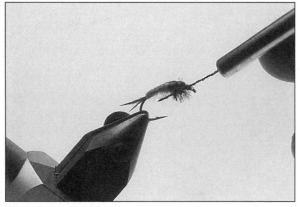

9. Use a dubbing teaser or bodkin to pick out dubbing giving a buggy appearance.

10. Finished Net Builder.

BARR STONEFLY NYMPH

John Barr

I started tying stonefly nymphs in the mid-70's with a simple approach: tie a fly that accurately imitated the color and movement of a natural. It occurred to me that big naturals were either a light golden stone color or basically dark. For movement, Charles Brook's use of hackle for the legs on his Brook's Stone seemed like a good idea. The use of a Ziploc bag for the back of the pattern to make it look juicy when it was wet was added later. The greatest influence on this fly came from the first fly tying book I bought, a first edition of

Polly Rosborough's, *Tying and Fishing the Fuzzy Nymph*. Polly's approach to blending hair and fur and their application to dubbed nymph bodies continues to influence my tying today. Although I have never had the pleasure of meeting Polly, I feel that he is my greatest tying mentor. The buggy, alive quality of my patterns should be credited to him.

The finished Barr Stonefly Nymph pattern has soft movement and looks like live bait in the water. My fishing friends and I have had years of success fishing it on streams throughout the West.

I have a favorite stream in Colorado which flows into a reservoir. In the spring, rainbows and cutts to 10 pounds run up this stream from the reservoir to spawn. Now, this stream doesn't have any big stoneflies in it, but it does have lots of baby crayfish. The way these big trout crunch the Barr Stonefly Nymph I am reasonably sure that it is being taken as a crayfish. Any pattern that can crossover in a trout's eye is fine with me.

BARR GOLDEN STONE

HOOK:	Tiemco 5263 or Dai-Riki 710 or equivalent, sizes 6-10
THREAD:	3/0 tan monocord
TAIL:	Ginger goose biot
BODY:	Cream coarse synthetic dubbing
BACK:	Plastic cut from Ziploc bag
LEGS:	Ginger hen hackle or poor grade rooster hackle
RIBBING:	3/0 mono

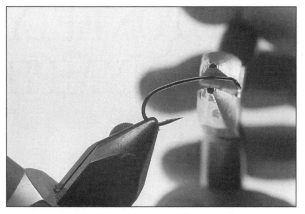

1. With the hook securely in the vise use pliers to bend the hook as shown.

2. Tie in a pair of goose biots for a forked tail as shown.

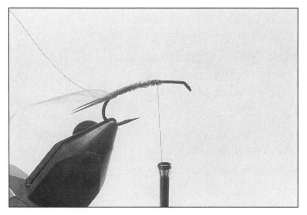

3. Tie in mono and cut Ziploc plastic strip at the rear of the fly.

4. After dubbing a tapered abdomen, secure the stem of a hen hackle for the legs.

5. Dub a thorax and use a dark felt tip pen to mottle the back of the fly.

6. Palmer the hen hackle through the thorax.

7. Pull the plastic strip to the eye and secure with thread.

8. Rib with the mono making progressively larger segments through the abdomen and forming a distinct thorax. Whip finish.

9. Darken the thread head with a felt tip pen.

10. Make a small cut in the plastic at the thorax to flare it.

11. Use a dubbing teaser or bodkin to pick out the dubbing and give it a more buggy appearance.

12. The finished Barr Golden Stone Nymph.

GOLDEN BURLAP NYMPH

Chuck Stranahan

I had scarcely paid my respects to Polly Rosborough at an ISE Angling Show in San Mateo a number of years ago when he grabbed one of the first Golden Burlap Nymphs from my hand, turned to a bystander and almost hollered, "Now there's a fish-producing fly!" The other fellow, a well-read but under-experienced angler, had been grilling Polly as to why his Golden Stone didn't have two wing pads. The garrulous Polly apparently had been, before my arrival at his tying station, mounting a staunch defense of his fuzzy, buggy looking nymphs. I didn't mean to enter the debate, but it was one of the most gratifying compliments I've ever received for my fly tying.

The Golden Burlap was born of a sense of proportion and nymph design gleaned from my two mentors, Cal Bird and Polly. The material choice, burlap dyed Antique Brass, available at most well-supplied yardage shops, was a natural. As Polly and I discussed after he had run his tormentor off, burlap is a fish catching material that is too often ignored. In the case of my nymph, it makes the fly.

Golden Stones are available in most of our western rivers and, I suspect, are more significant than the attention they receive. They are in the stream for a couple of years and are available to the trout year-round. When they molt, they are light in color, fragile and often drift along the bottom of the stream until eaten. The unmarked version of the Golden Burlap is one of my favorite general-purpose deep nymphs for the entire season. I usually confine my fishing of the darkened back variation to hatch and pre-hatch periods.

As I write this, it is a hot early August day on the Bitterroot River. Golden Stones have long since come and gone. Normally a fine dry fly stream, the Bitterroot has only grudgingly yielded anything on the surface for the past week. Two of my angling friends, Jerry Bliss and Phil Romans, have been doing well underneath, with the Golden Burlap out-producing all other flies by a wide margin. The fact that Jerry and Phil both know what they're doing could have something to do with their success. Still, they both attribute a lot to the fly.

Did they hit a Golden Stone molting cycle on the nose and luck out? Hard to say. The fact is that it works.

GOLDEN BURLAP NYMPH

HOOK:	Dai-Riki 710, Tiemco 5263 or equivalent, sizes 6-8
THREAD:	3/0 tan monocord
LEAD:	.025
TAIL:	Ringneck pheasant feathers
BODY:	Burlap dyed antique brass or gold, top of body is colored with a brown permanent felt marker
WINGCASE:	Section of white top turkey tail
HACKLE:	Natural mottled brown hen back or other large soft hackle

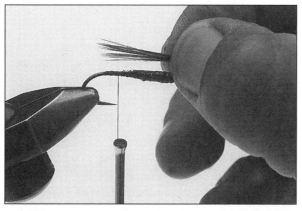

1. After weighting the middle third of the hook shank with .025 lead select fibers from a ringneck pheasant tail feather. Tail should be half the fly length.

2. Pull out a strand of burlap about 12 inches long.

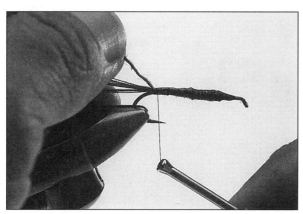

3. Tie in along the top of the fly as shown.

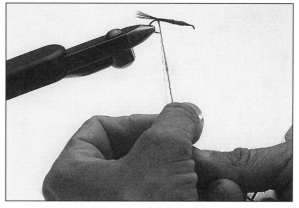

4. Hold the burlap and thread together and twist in the direction of the twist of the burlap fiber.

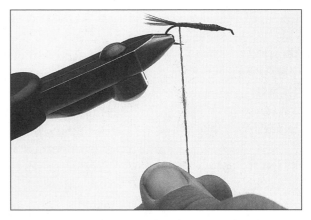

5. Illustrates what twisted burlap and thread looks like.

6. Roughen the burlap with the blunt edge of the scissors.

7. To segment abdomen, twist the burlap and wrap forward.

8. Segmented abdomen tied off but tag end of burlap is not trimmed.

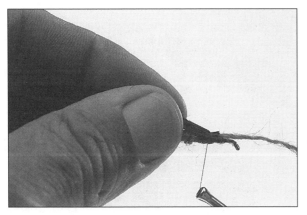

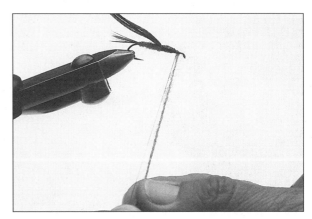

9. Tie in fibers from turkey tail for the wing case.

10. Wrap the burlap around the thread. Page 63, step 4.

11. Wrap the thorax from front to back then back to front without segmenting.

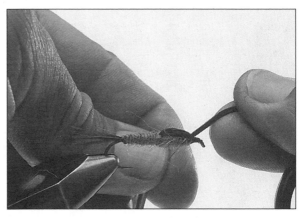

12. Pull the turkey fibers over and tie off to form the wing case.

13. Tie in the butt of the hen feather for the hackle.

14. Make 2 or 3 wraps of the hackle feather pulling the fibers back with each wrap.

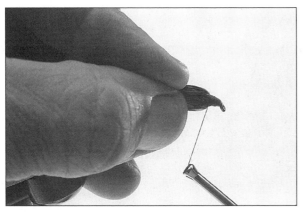

15. Pull the feathers back and secure with enough thread wraps to form the head as shown.

16. Whip finish.

17. Trim the top and bottom of the hackle fibers so that the legs formed are only to the right and left.

18. Color the back of the abdomen with a felt tip marker. Make one stroke only from the back to the front.

19. Top view of finished Golden Burlap Nymph.

20. Finished Golden Burlap Nymph.

GEORGE'S RUBBER LEG BROWN STONE

Jack Dennis

This fly was developed by George Anderson, who owns and operates the Yellowstone Angler Fly Shop in Livingston, Montana. During the second day of the 1989 Jackson Hole One Fly, George used this fly to catch 78 cutthroat trout and capture the individual championship for himself and the team championship for Simms-Lifelink. This accomplishment should give you an idea of both the effectiveness and durability of this fly.

Wherever stoneflies are found, you can bet this pattern will work. The woven body, hair thorax and rubber legs all contribute to a buggy impression of life. If you have wanted to try tying woven body flies, this is an ideal pattern to start off with, since it is the easy to master. While there are a number of different techniques for weaving fly bodies, the overhand knot weave is one method you can use to tie a variety of flies.

Look around in a fabric shop sometime and you will be amazed at the variety of yarns and such that can be used to tie flies. Many of these materials are ideal for weaving fly bodies. If you try weaving with chenille, don't be discouraged when it breaks. Most yarns are sufficiently stronger and should be used instead of chenille.

If you are interested in learning more about the art of weaving flies. George Grant's books, *The Master Fly Weaver* and *Montana Trout Flies* are excellent references.

GEORGE'S RUBBER LEG BROWN STONE

HOOK:	DaiRiki 710 or equivalent, sizes 4-10
THREAD:	3/0 tan or brown monocord
LEAD:	.030
TAIL & LEGS:	Med. size white or brown rubber legs
ABDOMEN:	One strand brown, one strand tan wool yarn, woven
THORAX:	Hare's ear natural color or tan squirrel blend

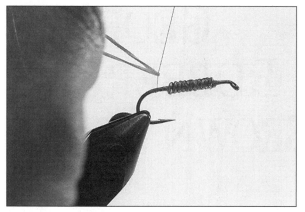

1. After heavily weighting the shank as shown, wrap rubber leg material around the strand of thread, secure and form the tail.

2. Tie the dark yarn to the far side of the hook.

3. Tie the light colored yarn to the near side of the hook.

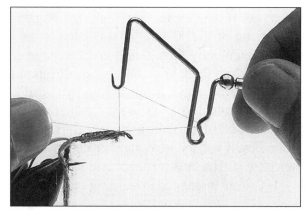

4. Bring the thread to the front, whip finish and cut the thread.

5. Turn the vise to point the hook straight at you. The dark colored yarn is always in front of the light colored yarn.

6. Make a simple overhand knot as shown.

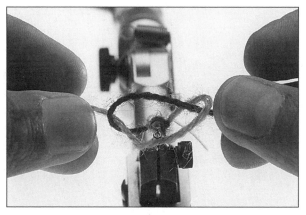

7. Begin to close knot. Notice that the light colored yarn in the knot is always under the eye of the hook and the dark color is always on top of the eye of the hook.

8. Top view of the weaving process showing the configuration of the knot as it closes.

9. After weaving into the thorax, reattach the thread, tie off and trim the yarn and attach rubber legs to the far and near side of the hook in the same manner that the tail was done at the rear.

10. Dub the thorax, separating the front and rear rubber legs. Whip finish.

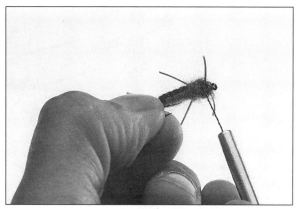

11. Trim the tail and legs to desired length.

12. Pick out thorax with dubbing teaser or bodkin.

13. Finished George's Rubber Leg Brown Stone.

RANGITAIKI RUBBER LEGS

Jack Dennis

It was 1984 and a cold rain fell upon New Zealand's Rangitaiki River. I remember it as if it was yesterday. We had helicoptered into what was to be a four day float through the steep dark walls of a Rangitaiki canyon. I was with an old friend and fellow guide, Tom Kemper, a friend of his by the name of Jack McKenzie and two close fishing companions of mine, Skip Brittenham and Ken August. There was just enough rain to freshen the landscape but not muddy the river.

Although the light was poor, we could spot fish feeding in water from four to eight feet deep. After about three hours of trying every nymph in our boxes and not getting down to the fish, we resorted to the guide's recommended choice of an extremely heavily weighted stonefly designed by Tom. I swear that it had a Mepps spinner wrapped inside the body as it hit the water with a tremendous splash and sank immediately to the necessary depth. No need for split shots on this baby! These trout are very wiley and it is impossible to approach them with anything less than a 14 foot leader, a true casting exhibition with this heavy nymph. Before the day was over, all of us would have bruises on the backs of our necks and heads.

As the day wore on, it was evident that Tom's fly worked. Skip took a nine pound rainbow that did cartwheels across the water, stripping his line and most of the backing from the spool of his reel. By the end of the day many hefty rainbows had been boated on Tom's brown weighted stone. What surprised me was that the flies were fished at an absolute dead drift and if the fish saw the fly, gave it a good look and didn't take it, that was it, no second chance. It occurred to me that the materials used to tie the fly gave only a minimal image of a live moving insect.

Later that night as the rain pounded against the side of the tent, an idea came to mind. It was to add paper thin rubber legs to Tom's pattern and give it some life. At that time they didn't have very thin rubber legs available for tying. I had to take a razor blade and cut thick rubber legs down to thin wisps. I then colored them black with a magic marker. Tom's Brown Stone with thin black rubber legs became the Rangitaiki Rubber Legs. The movement of the rubber legs seems to excite even cautious New Zealand trout into smashing the fly.

The Rangitaiki Rubber Legs' ultimate triumph came in 1988 during the filming of a segment for Larry Schoenborn's program, *Fishing the West*. Guide Tony Entwhistle had attempted to catch one large brown trout for three seasons. It resided in a deep tea colored pool in a high mountain meadow stream surrounded by willows. That brown ate my Rangitaiki Rubber Legs and became the highlight of the program. It weighed in at just under eight pounds.

You can tie the Rangitaiki Rubber Legs in sizes as small as 16 and as large as 2. You can also vary the color from browns and olives to black. The choice is yours; adapt it to the stoneflies in your region.

RANGITAIKI RUBBER LEGS

HOOK:	Dai-Riki 710 or equivalent, sizes 2-12
THREAD:	3/0 black or brown monocord
LEAD:	.035 or to hook size
BODY:	Blend of mohair wool + sparkle synthetic yarn to get a brownish color dubbing or Scintilla #25 Orangish Sepia, #'s 14 & 24 acceptable substitutes
ANTENNAE, LEGS, TAILS:	Size small round or square black rubber legs
RIBBING:	Med. copper wire
WINGCASE:	Turkey tail

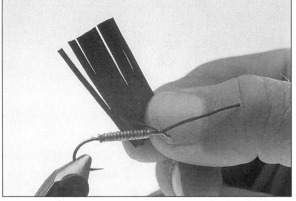

1. After leading the hook as shown, tie in a pair of rubber legs not separated for the forward antennae.

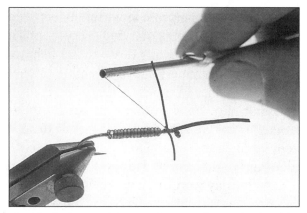

2. Tie in forward legs and secure by ' X-ing' with the thread.

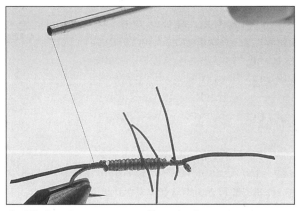

3. Tie in other two sets of legs in the same manner and undivided tail rubber leg material.

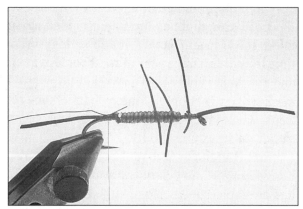

4. Tie in ribbing.

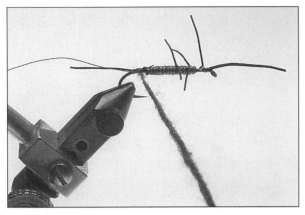

5. Dub the abdomen forward.

6. Cut out a section of turkey tail feather for the wing case.

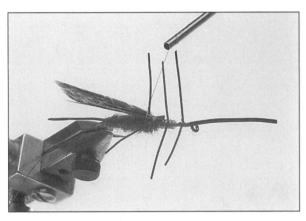

7. Tie in the turkey feather as shown.

8. Dub the thorax equally separating the legs as shown.

9. Pull the turkey section forward to form the wing case.

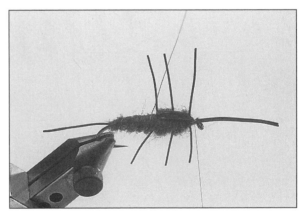

10. Rib the body forward all the way to the front.

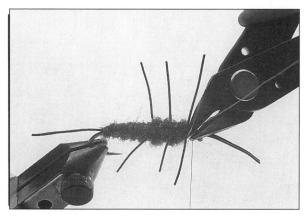

11. Clip the wire and whip finish. Pick out the dubbing just as we've done in a number of other nymphs to give it a buggy appearance.

12. The finished Rangitaiki Rubber Legs. Antennae and tail should be separated as seen in color plate.

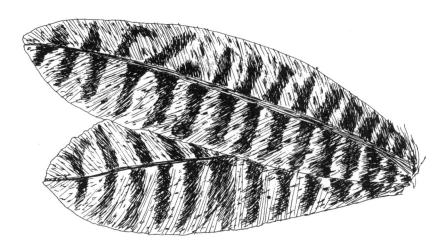

COPPER CREEPER

Jack Dennis

The origin of this easy to tie nymph is Colorado, where it is called a Brassie. If you tie the body of the Copper Creeper with a heavier gauge wire than is normally found on the Brassie, there is a very distinct segmentation to it. In addition, the heavier wire can often alleviate the need to put weight on the leader to get the fly down quickly. When fishing shallow riffs or runs during midge activity, it is frustrating to have the weight or leader hang-up on the bottom and spook the fish.

Chuck Stranahan of Hamilton, Montana has an interesting variation for the body. He uses a Cal Bird dubbing tool to twist two to six strands of light wire, then mixes the colors of the wire to get a variegated look. The results are very impressive.

Although the Copper Creeper can be tied in sizes 18 or smaller, a size 16 will probably do the trick for you in most situations. Be sure to use a heavy wire hook. Don't use dry fly hooks because the wire is too light and they will bend when they snag on the bottom. Your next good sized fish will once again straighten the hook.

Peacock herl is a good material for the Copper Creeper's head. However, you can substitute ostrich herl, natural fur, Antron blend dubbing or a small soft hackle and probably do fine.

The Copper Creeper works well whenever you see midges on the water. It doesn't make any difference whether the fish are rising to adults or not. Simply work to the head of the run where the midges have been emerging and more often than not you will get real busy.

This pattern is a must to have when fishing spring creeks. It usually works best when fished dead drift, but on certain streams, such as the Firehole River, it produces well when fished down and across on a swing.

For a little more than the cost of the hooks, you can tie a big supply of these deadly flies in short order. Make sure to add it to your arsenal of flies.

COPPER CREEPER

HOOK:	Dai-Riki 070 or equivalent, sizes 16-20
THREAD:	8/0 black
BODY:	Heavy copper wire
HEAD:	Peacock herl or substitute ostrich herl or Scintilla dubbing

NOTE: A single goose biot can be used for the body instead of the copper wire. Glue the thread underbody before wrapping the biot. This makes it extremely durable.

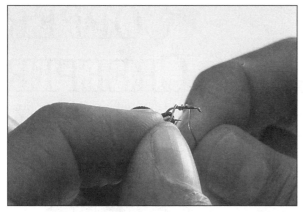

1. Make an underbody of thread on the hook shank. Using both hands wrap the copper wire forward as shown.

2. Use smooth jaw forceps to flatten the fore and aft cut ends of the copper wire.

3. Attach a single strand of herl for the head.

4. Wrap the herl around the thread as shown.

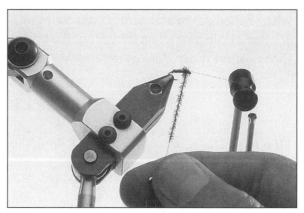

5. Form a dubbing loop with the Dubbit tool and spin forming a single strand of herl chenille.

6. Make 3 to 6 turns of herl to form the head. Whip finish the head.

7. Finished Copper Creeper.

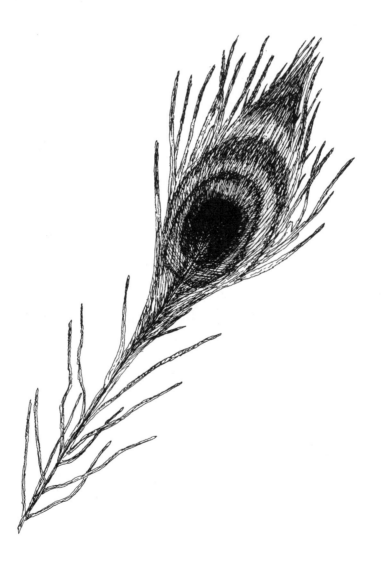

BEAD HEAD PHEASANT TAIL NYMPH

Joe Burke

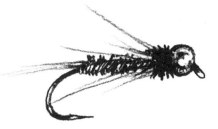

When Mike Lawson drove over to Jackson Hole from his home in St. Anthony, Idaho to tie flies for this manual one of the first things he said was:

"I know you are getting down to the wire on this book, but there was a series of flies that was so deadly for our clients on the Henry's Fork and Madison this summer that you really should find room for it. They are the bead head flies. You can put a bead head on any nymph and it immediately becomes more effective.

"I think they work for a few obvious reasons. First, they sink fast so you can cover more of the bottom. Second, they sink head down, so even on the drift they act like a jig. Lastly, and I think most important, the bead looks like an air bubble in front of the fly and the trout seem to key on that.

"My guides went through every single one of them I had in the shop. Some standard nymphs like the Hare's Ear and Prince Nymph worked well, as did a Serendipity with a bead replacing the tuft of deer hair on the head. A real favorite with the guides was a Bead Head Pheasant Tail Nymph with a peacock herl thorax behind the bead head. I'll tell you one thing, the shop will be loaded with bead heads next year because the word is out on them."

A fly tier from Denmark named Theo Bakelaar introduced the bead head flies to the U.S. in 1991 at the FFF Conclave in West Yellowstone, Montana. If you happened to be there, you might remember him. He was the guy with his head painted gold. No kidding! Umpqua Feather Merchants decided to feature Theo's flies. Ken Menard of Umpqua shared this:

"Initially we had trouble selling them to shops because of the strange names Theo gave his patterns. Danger Baby and Theo's Dream are not exactly household names when fly shops get around to ordering flies. One pattern, the Hare's Ear Shaggy did get some commercial interest. As soon as anglers tried them the word spread like wildfire. We got reports of guys having the best angling days of their lives with bead heads. We would hear of people who couldn't believe the fly made that much of a difference, so they would switch to some other proven nymph pattern. Action would stop so they would go back to the bead heads once again and the action would continue.

"At Umpqua, we use a 24K gold plated bead which does not tarnish like the brass beads do. The shiny round head has the same sparkle no matter what angle the fish sees it from."

The Bead Head Pheasant Tail Nymph is a last minute addition to this manual. With the remarkable bead head tales that area guides are reporting it would be a shame to overlook it. Try using a bead head on your favorite nymph pattern.

BEAD HEAD PHEASANT TAIL NYMPH

HOOK:	Dai-Riki 070 or equivalent, sizes 10-20
THREAD:	8/0 brown
TAIL:	Pheasant tail feather fibers
BODY:	Pheasant tail feather fibers
RIBBING:	Med. copper wire
THORAX:	Peacock herl
LEGS:	Tips of fibers of pheasant tail feather
HEAD:	Small gold bead

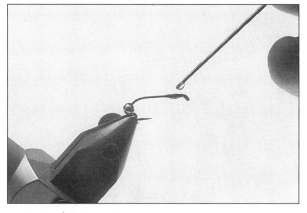

1. Before putting the hook in the vise slip the bead over the bend of the hook. Put the hook in the vise and whip finish thread behind the eye and glue.

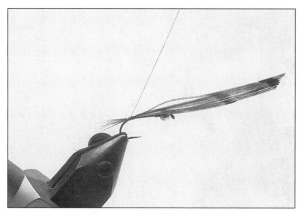

2. Slide the bead forward over the glued area; re-attach the thread and tie in pheasant tail fibers as a tail. Do not cut tag ends.

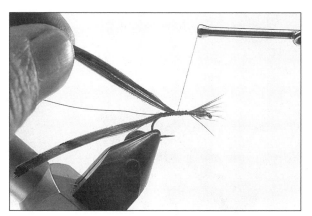

3. Tie in wire for ribbing. Tie in pheasant tail fibers with the tips forward. By wrapping thread over some of these fibers you can begin to taper the body.

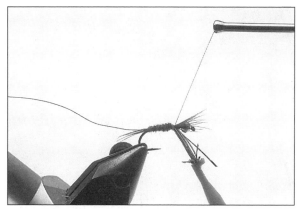

4. Wrap the butt segment of the pheasant fibers of the tail forward as shown.

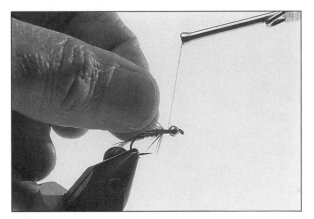

6. Divide the pheasant tail fibers with thread to form right and left legs as shown.

7. Attach 1 to 3 peacock herl fibers and twist around the thread.

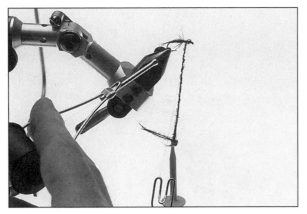

8. Secure the herl tips with hackle pliers so they don't untwist and form a dubbing loop with the Dubbit. Close top of loop with thread.

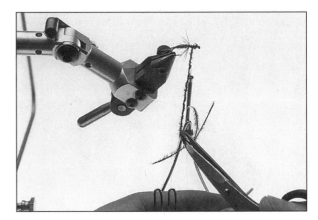

9. Trim tag ends of herl, loop will spin much easier.

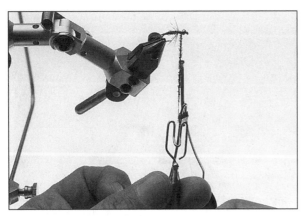

10. Spin the Dubbit to form a peacock herl chenille.

11. Wrap the thorax with the chenille and whip finish.

12. Finished Bead Head Pheasant Tail Nymph.

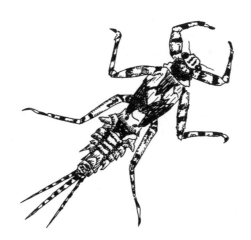

HAIR HACKLE NYMPH

Scott Sanchez

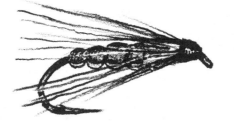

The Mite style fly, such as the Sandy Mite, was the standard wet fly used in the Rockies during the 40's and 50's. Like so many older patterns, their popularity has diminished, but their effectiveness has not.

These flies were designed to fish in riffle water common to many Western trout streams. George Grant in his excellent book, *The Master Fly Weaver*, explains that the stiffer hair hackle on these flies actually gives more action than softer materials gives when worked against strong currents. These flies are sold by the Pott Fly Company and are still popular with many old timers.

Being curious about the fish catching abilities of these flies, I tried tying some. The patented Pott style of weaving hair hackles and bodies makes a very durable fly but it is very time consuming to tie. After some experimentation with both methods and materials, I concocted a hair hackle substitute for the Sandy Mite that gave me a segmented body without weaving. The belly color is basically done by tying multiple wing cases and the hair hackle is a modified bullet head.

The fish catching ability of these new Hair Hackle Nymphs is outstanding. During caddis and small stonefly emergences they outfish many standard patterns.

Horse hair and boar hair used in the traditional Sandy Mite are not commonly available materials these days. Reasonable substitutes for the hackle are elk mane, bucktail, squirrel tail, moose mane, deer shoulder or Fishair. Elk mane, Fishair or embroidery floss works well for the body. These can be combined in a variety of ways to create a number of exciting combinations.

Hopefully, with this simplified tying method you will take the opportunity to tie and fish some Hair Hackle Nymphs. They are as durable and effective as the original Mite series of flies. The pattern chosen here is similar to the original Sandy Mite, which is possibly the most popular of the Mite series of flies.

HAIR HACKLE NYMPH

HOOK:	Dai-Riki 075 or equivalent, sizes 8-16
THREAD:	8/0 brown
HACKLE COLLAR:	Stacked elk mane hair; can use squirrel tail in small sizes
BODY:	Sandy color cotton embroidery thread woven with 4 strands of orange flat waxed nylon tying thread

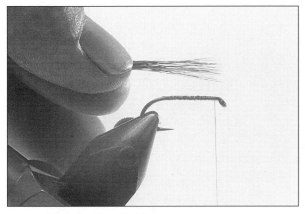

1. After covering the hook shank with a layer of thread, measure the stacked elk mane with tips forward from the eye of the hook to just beyond the bend.

2. Tie the elk mane just behind the eye as shown with the tips facing forward.

3. Push the hair 360 degrees around the hook shank with your fingers. Secure with thread and trim the butts.

4. Tie in the embroidery thread and the four strands of flat waxed nylon just behind the elk mane. Wrap the thread to the butt of the fly.

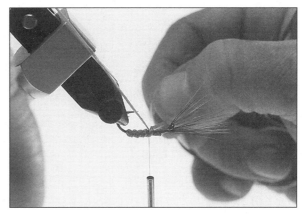

5. Put the hook in the vise upside down. Twist the embroidery thread

6. Pull the four strand nylon back with the left hand then pull the embroidery thread over in front of it with the right hand.

7. Pull the four strand nylon forward over the embroidery yarn.

8. Secure the four strand nylon with two turns of tying thread.

9. Repeat this weaving process to 1 to 2 eye lengths behind the hair hackle as shown.

10. Stroke the collar back to get a 360 degree distribution of the hair hackle.

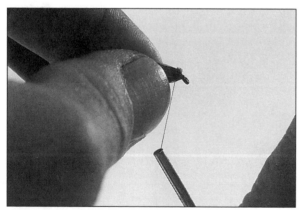

11. Secure with thread wraps and whip finish. Glue the head with clear nail polish.

12. Finished Hair Hackle Nymph

EMERGERS, CRIPPLES, & STILLBORNS

PARACHUTE MIDGE EMERGER

Gary Willmott

When I am guiding the same stretch of the river on a regular basis, I get a good chance to see how trout become progressively more selective. This day-to-day progression can be measured by refusals. Clients will put a good presentation of a proven pattern over a fish; it will drift up and give a look, followed by a big "No, I don't think so."

While searching for a pattern to cut down on this refusal phenomenon, Scott Sanchez and I developed the Parachute Midge Emerger (PME).

My first field test of the PME was during an Upper Snake River excursion with a couple of guide buddies, Paul Bruun and Tom Montgomery. We threw the PME over fish which would refuse all other patterns, but they would grab the PME every time. Over the past few seasons, I have found that the PME is deadly when used on lakes and ponds where trout are cruising and sipping chironomids. It is also a sure thing to use on those tough scum suckers that work the back eddies of the Green River below Flaming Gorge Reservoir.

The PME is an easy pattern to tie. It can be tied in sizes 16 through 22, but size 18 is by far the best. The colors I most often use for the dubbed body are gray, black and red (works especially well in lakes) and all of them are ribbed with Krystal Flash. I have fished a PME without ribbing and it doesn't perform well. Rainbow colored Krystal Flash is my usual choice, but I have also had good luck with red, peacock and root beer colors. The PME can be tied on a down eye hook, but I prefer to tie it on a straight eye hook.

When you tie it on, use a loop knot, so that the rear of the fly sinks below the surface like a natural midge emerger does. It will hang in the surface film if you grease only the wing and hackle, and not the body. Give this pattern a try when fish are sipping midges and I'm sure you will be as pleased as I am with its performance.

PARACHUTE MIDGE EMERGER

HOOK:	Dai-Riki 310 or equivalent, sizes 16-22
THREAD:	8/0 black
BODY:	Scintilla #46 Peacockle dubbing or other sparkle blend peacock color dubbing
RIBBING:	Rainbow color Krystal Flash
WING:	White poly, white Antron, or white calf body hair
HACKLE:	Grizzly or dun neck hackle feather

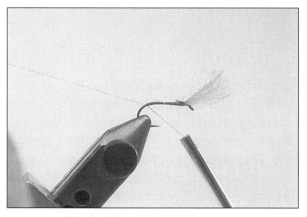

1. After attaching the wing as shown attach a single strand of Krystal Flash.

2. Dub the body with the suggested dubbing material or with wraps of peacock herl.

3. After dubbing with the taper as shown, rib the fly to just behind the wing.

4. Tie in a single hackle feather.

5. Make 2 to 5 turns of hackle behind the wing. Tie off and whip finish.

6. The finished Parachute Midge Emerger.

MINIMAL MAYFLY

Ralph Headrick

This fly was developed by Jackson Hole fishing guide Ralph Headrick. Not only has Ralph developed fly patterns based on his guiding experience, but he and his fellow guide friend Paul Bruun have developed and built the South Fork Skiff drift boat. Due to its ease of handling and the comfort it affords clients, it is the boat of choice of many area guides.

"Because of the demand for our South Fork Skiff, my fly tying time has become quite limited," Ralph says, "I wanted an uncomplicated fly that could be tied quickly, represent a number of insect forms, and of course, catch fish.

"About four years ago I fished the South Fork in early autumn. Typically, the water is low this time of year and the fish have been hammered all summer, so they are very cautious. Although there were pods of trout selectively feeding on emerging *Baetis*, approaching them and then fooling them with an artificial was tough. I examined some naturals, and paid close attention to size and silhouette. They were much more subtle than most patterns I had. The Harrop Hair Wing Dun was the closest imitator in my fly selection and I did fool a few of the trout using it. The Minimal Mayfly is really a simplified version of Rene's fly."

Ralph has a few tying tips to add to the pattern's versatility. "If you use a short wing you have a mayfly emerger; a longer wing represents a dun; and longer yet is a caddis. However, I feel it's truest niche is as an emerger during Blue Wing Olive and Pale Morning Dun hatches."

When Bear McKinney, another area guide and advocate of the Minimal Mayfly, was asked how he thought this pattern worked he started to drool like a Pavlovian dog, smiled and replied, "Oh boy!"

Simple fly patterns such as the Minimal Mayfly are usually not available in fly shops because they have little customer appeal. "I didn't tie this pattern to catch customers, I tied it to catch fish," Ralph says. "And it's fun to catch fish on such a simple fly."

MINIMAL MAYFLY

HOOK:	Dai-Riki 300, 305 or equivalent, sizes 12-22
THREAD:	6/0 or 8/0 prewaxed, color to match body
TAIL:	Stiff hackle fibers, color to match or contrast body
BODY:	Very fine poly dubbing, color to match natural
WING:	Natural deer body hair, fine texture

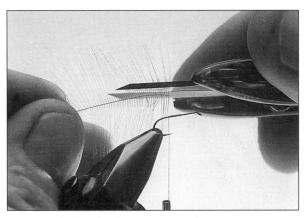

1. Attach the thread mid shank and wrap to above the hook point. Trim out hackle fibers for the tail.

2. Tie in hackle fiber tail but do not flare with the wraps of thread; the length should be 1/2 the shank length.

3. Dub a slightly tapered body with a fatter thorax as shown almost 1/3 shank length back from the hook eye.

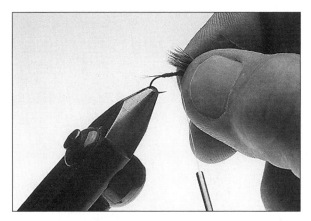

4. After cutting, cleaning and stacking the deer hair wing, measure the wing to the desired length for either the emerger or dun.

5. Secure the deer hair with several progressively tighter wraps of thread. The hair should not spin around the hook. Note the length for a dun is just to the hook point as shown here.

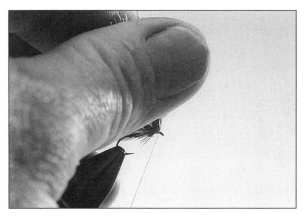

6. Pull up the butt ends and wrap the thread in front of them, then trim the butts even.

7. Whip finish in front of the trimmed butts.

8. A side and front view of the finished Minimal Mayfly.

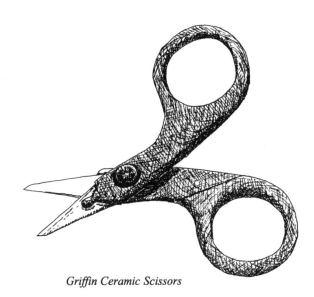

Griffin Ceramic Scissors

QUIGLEY CRIPPLE

Joe Burke

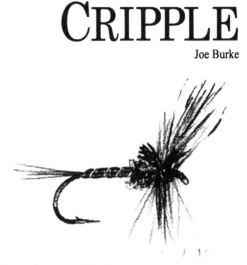

The Quigley Cripple and the Barr Emerger are two fly patterns which I am never without when I head for my favorite streams. The Quigley Cripple is the creation of a Californian named Bob Quigley. I have never met Bob, but a friend of mine, Chuck Stranahan recalls his acquaintance with this innovative tier:

"Bob moved to California's Fall River area as a young man. He was from the Bay Area and had a grasp of fundamental tying skills, as well as skills he developed through the tutelage of many of the great Bay area tiers of the 60's. Headquartered out of Rick's Lodge, his was the first fly shop on the famous Fall River. I became well acquainted with him when I opened Hat Creek Anglers in 1979. I remember him as a friendly competitor who happened to have a great natural talent for tying. Materials just seemed to flow through his fingers with grace.

"The Cripple evolved from an experience Bob had fishing a small Humpy on Hat Creek during an evening mayfly hatch. He observed that the Humpy was more effective the more chewed up it got. His inquisitive mind then took over. Bob's first attempts on the vise tried to imitate how the back part of the deer hair hump was chopped and the body material was frayed. He used marabou for the tail and abdomen; deer hair for flotation and a visible wing; and lastly a few sparse wraps of hackle to give stability and create essential dimples in the water around the fly.

"Bob correctly reasoned that the trout were taking mayflies which were partially emerged and then fried in the hot California sun before becoming adults. His emergers were later modified by meticulous and talented area tiers such as Bob Cockcroft, Gary Warren and Mike Monroe (Paratilt). The Fall River school of tiers has gotten little credit in literature for it's influence on the many spring creek patterns which are so widely used throughout the West today."

There is not one river, stream or spring creek where this fly has not been productive for me. I have found it to be a good crossover pattern during mayfly, midge and even caddis activity. But, it's truest niche is as a mayfly emerger.

Tied in a size 10 green color, it is highly effective during the June Western Green Drake hatch on the Henry's Fork. If Pale Morning Duns, Blue Winged Olives or late season Mahogany Duns are around, a size 16 or 18 brown or olive Quigley Cripple is my fly of choice.

I tie the Quigley Cripple in a couple of variations depending on size. For a size 16 or smaller, when I am trying to imitate midges and small mayflies, I use a chopped hackle fiber tail and thread abdomen. I usually rib the abdomen with white horsehair to give a segmented appearance. Try pheasant tail fibers or goose biot for the abdomen on smaller sizes.

When imitating bigger mayflies, such as Green Drakes and Brown Drakes, say sizes 10 through 14, I use marabou from the stems of dyed grizzly saddle hackles for the tail; dub a body and segment it with floss; and use peacock herl or an Antron blend dubbing such as Scintilla for the thorax. The deer hair wing and wingcase are on all sizes, as is the hackle.

The Quigley Cripple works in so many situations. Unfortunately, it is not available in many fly shops, so be sure to learn to tie it.

GREEN DRAKE QUIGLEY CRIPPLE

HOOK:	Dai-Riki 305 or equivalent, size 10-12
THREAD:	6/0 olive
TAIL:	Olive dyed grizzly marabou
ABDOMEN:	Olive synthetic dubbing or; wrap body with dyed grizzly marabou as Jay Buchner does on the Snake River Muddler, page 232
RIBBING:	Single strand yellow silk floss
THORAX:	2-3 peacock herls or dark dubbing
WING CASE:	Natural deer hair
FOREWING:	Natural deer hair
HACKLE:	Olive dyed grizzly saddle or hackle

MAHOGANY QUIGLEY CRIPPLE

HOOK:	Tiemco 100, 101, Dai-Riki 305, 310 or equivalent, sizes 10-20
THREAD:	8/0 brown
TAIL:	Stiff brown hackle fibers, clipped
ABDOMEN:	Tying thread
RIBBING:	White horsehair or 8/0 thread
THORAX:	Brown fine poly dubbing or brown Scintilla dubbing
WINGCASE:	Natural deer hair
FOREWING:	Natural deer hair
HACKLE:	Dun or dun dyed grizzly neck hackle

Title: Mahogany Quigley Cripple

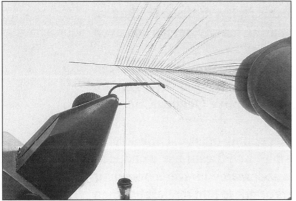

1. Tie in tail with wraps of thread on the rear 2/3 of the hook shank. Do not flare the hackle tail.

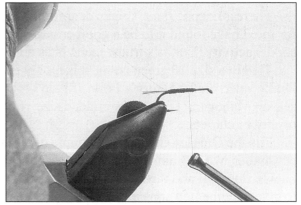

2. Trim the tail as shown and attach the ribbing.

3. Create an abdomen with the tying thread and rib forward.

4. Dub a thorax.

5. Finished thorax showing proportions.

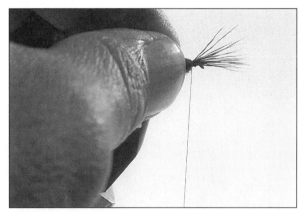

6. Attached stacked, cleaned deer hair over the eye of the hook. Be sure not to let it rotate around the hook.

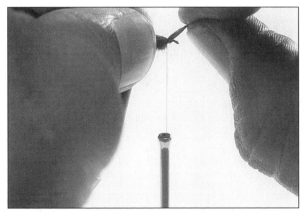

7. With your fingers you can wiggle the wing for placement.

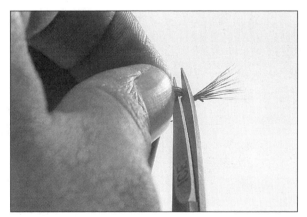

8. Trim the butts to form a wing case over the thorax.

9. Prepare a hackle feather to be attached between the wing case and the wing.

10. Make 2 to 3 wraps of hackle behind the wing and 1 wrap in front of the wing; whip finish.

11. Finished Quigley Cripple.

BARR EMERGER

Joe Burke

The Barr Emerger and Quigley Cripple are two of my all-time favorite fly patterns. They have accounted for more of the trout I have caught over the past ten years than any other patterns.

A product of Dr. John Barr, a dentist from Boulder, Colorado, John recounts its development:

"Back in the 70's I used to fish a lot on the spring creeks around Livingston, Montana. On one of these outings the fishing was particularly tough. I caught a couple on nymphs, but overall the fish were uncatchable. I watched in frustration as numerous nice trout sipped what looked like specks on the water. The specks turned out to be the emerging PMD's coming out of their nymphal shucks. That night back at the motel, I tied my first Barr Emerger. The rear portion of the pattern represents the nymphal shuck and the front portion represents the emerging adult. With the exception of size and color, I haven't changed a thing about it since. In fact, it worked so well that George Anderson asked if he could carry the pattern in his shop, the Yellowstone Angler."

I first used this pattern on Livingston's spring creeks at the recommendation of George Anderson. Probably because I was in one of my early morning, pre-fishing trances, I didn't listen well to George and thought the fly was a nymph. Until corrected by John Barr, I always thought the name of the fly was the Dr. Barr Nymph. I only tied the fly like the color of the ones I had purchased from George and fished it like a nymph.

My fishing buddy, Dennis Butcher and I have had many great days nymphing with the "Doc" on the Madison River. We would stick fish all day long, smile and say, "The doctor makes another house call." The Madison supports great numbers of Baetis mayfly nymphs and small free living caddis which look just like the Barr.

It hasn't been until the last few seasons that I have fished the Barr as an emerger. Only through trial and error fly selection while fishing to fussy trout, did the lights go on. I was amazed when those fussy no-take-ems became first cast eaters.

When I related this story to Dr. John Barr, he laughed. He said that he does tie his pattern on wet fly hooks and weights the leader to fish it as a nymph sometimes, but he feels it is more effective when fished as a floating emerger. "I tie it on a dry fly hook in sizes 16 through 20 for Pale Morning Dun emergence, and sizes 18 through 22 for *Baetis*," John says. "It also works very well in Colorado in the summer when the little yellow stoneflies are hatching. All you need to do is adjust the size and color for the hatch.

"The Barr Emerger is a great cross-over pattern. I have unfailing success using it when trout are sipping midges. I swing the fly into the rise form and let it hang there. The fish don't hesitate to grab it. Because these downstream takes are so hard you have to tie the Emerger on a stout wet fly hook, as a dry fly hook will straighten out. I have found the best color combination to use in a midge hatch is an olive abdomen and dun thorax."

Dr. John Barr, your Barr Emerger, a.k.a. Dr. Barr Nymph is a winner. I was fortunate enough to appear on both the May/June '91 and April '92 covers of *Fly Rod and Reel* magazine, and both fish I am pictured with were caught on the "Doc", one fished as an emerger, one fished as a nymph. I love this fly!

BLUE WING OLIVE BARR EMERGER

HOOK:	DRY - Tiemco 101, Dai-Riki 310 or equivalent, sizes 16-20
	WET - Tiemco 2457, Dai-Riki 135 or equivalent, sizes 14-18
THREAD:	8/0 dun color
TAIL:	Clipped stiff brown hackle fibers
ABDOMEN:	Fine olive dubbing
THORAX:	Fine dun colored dubbing
WINGCASE:	Dun hackle fibers
LEGS:	Dun hackle fibers

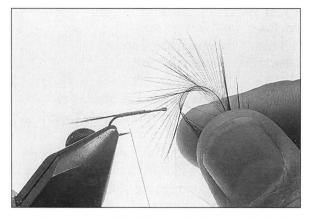

1. Tie in a hackle fiber tail, the length isn't important. Do not flare with too tight of thread wraps.

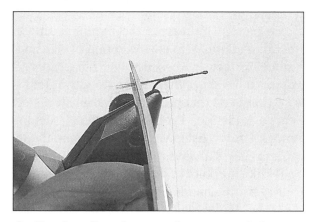

2. Cut the tail as shown to form a nymphal shuck.

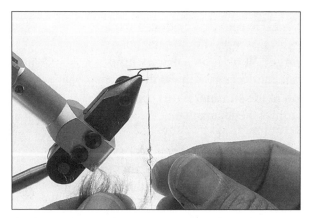

3. Sparsely dub the tying thread.

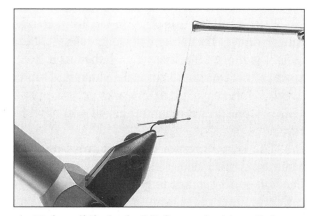

4. Dub a slight body 2/3 forward with a slight taper.

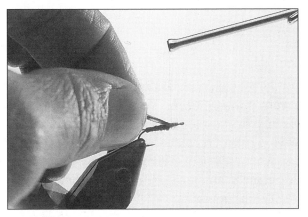

5. Attach hackle fibers as shown for the wing case and legs.

6. Sparsely dub the thread with the thorax dubbing.

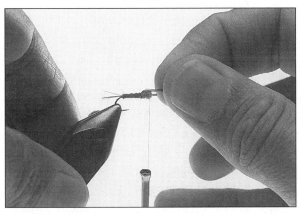

7. After dubbing the thorax slightly fatter than the abdomen, pull the hackle fibers forward to form a wing case.

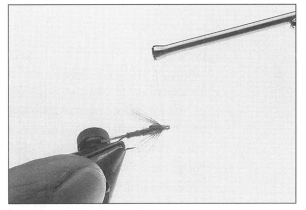

8. Separate the hackle fibers with your fingers and with thread wraps to form right and left pairs of legs as shown.

9. Trim the legs to desired length as shown.

10. The finished Barr Emerger.

ALL ROUNDER CADDIS PUPA

John Barr

I have used the All Rounder Caddis Pupa on rivers throughout the West with excellent results. It has worked on hatching caddis in colors ranging from black to light tan.

About seven or eight years ago I was fishing Montana's famous Bighorn River. The fish were really on emerging caddis and I was using a pattern with an Antron casing, which was soon stripped clean by the hungry fish. It worked just as well without the Antron as it did with it. This led me to realize that even though Antron doesn't hurt, it really isn't that significant either.

When the trout are on emerging caddis, they are very aggressive and not too selective toward pattern color or composition. If it has the silhouette and movement of an emerging caddis, it works. I have looked at the All Rounder Caddis Pupa in an aquarium to get an idea of what the trout is looking at. It's swimming movement and profile are perfect.

Before a known caddis hatch, I rig the All Rounder Caddis Pupa with a split shot, cast it upstream or cast it across stream and let it dead drift. I don't like to tie my nymphs with weight on the hook shank because I think that they float more naturally if the weight is on the leader. When trout begin to rise and bulge, I like to use the swing and hang technique (see Barr Emerger). Expect some savage rips with this technique.

Like all of the flies in the All Rounder Series, the Caddis Pupa is extremely easy to tie, durable and adapts well to a variety of hatch situations. This and all of my other patterns which are featured in this book are commercially available from Umpqua Feather Merchants.

ALL ROUNDER CADDIS PUPA

HOOK:	Tiemco 2457 or Dai-Riki 135, sizes 12-16
THREAD:	8/0 olive
BODY:	Brown/olive synthetic dubbing such as Scintilla
BACK:	Plastic cut from Ziploc bag
RIBBING:	4X mono
WINGPADS:	Black rabbit fur
LEGS & ANTENNAE:	Brown Hungarian partridge body feather fibers

1. Attach the mono ribbing as shown.

2. Tie in a strip of cut Ziploc bag.

3. Dub the thread for the body.

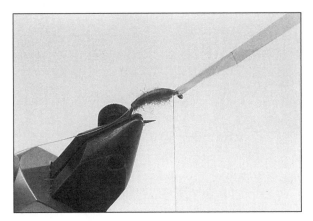

4. After dubbing a tapered body pull the plastic forward and secure with wraps of thread as shown.

5. Rib with the mono.

6. Attach a few fibers from a partridge body feather to the bottom of the hook for the legs and antennae.

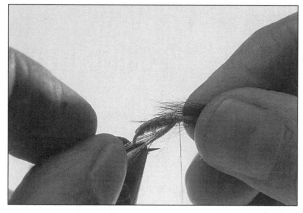

7. Push a clump of rabbit hair into the front of hook and tie down with the thread. Tips of this hair shouldn't go beyond the hook point. Whip finish.

8. The finished All Rounder Caddis Pupa.

CHUCK'S TWITCH-PAUSE NYMPH

Chuck Stranahan

John Eustice sat at the front of my pram, his retrieve rhythm accelerating with every boiling fish, every miss, every hookup. We were in the midst of a "caddis grab" on northern California's Fall River. Caddisflies were thick on the gunwales and oars, in our hair, under our glasses, and even crawling up our noses. Big trout were slamming the emergers with abandon and ignoring the adults.

John endured my chronic nagging to slow his retrieve speed with good humor. When he could control it he hooked fish, but if he speeded up, he didn't.

I finally told him, "John, with me. By the number. Cast...drift...twitch-pause...twitch-pause..." The incantation worked, and worked so well that it ruined a night's sleep, as he couldn't get it out of his head.

He called to set another trip date a couple of weeks later. When I answered the phone he responded "Twitch-pause...twitch-pause..." And the flies we used, which I used to call mossworms or caddis emergers, became known as Twitch-Pause Nymphs.

The flies are simple to tie, have segmented bodies and proportions which mimic the natural caddis. The trailing throat of soft hackle offers enough action to simulate the action of the natural. They look right in the water and have stood the test of time.

The body material of crewel embroidery wool can be found in a full spectrum of colors from any good yarn shop. You can match the exact requirements of any hatch you fish from the stock colors available. Lime green, avocado green, rusty brown, and tan with a slight pinkish cast do well for me as general purpose colors.

Keep the hen saddle throat sparse; it should be about twice body length and trail under the body. If it is too full, the fly will invert in the water. Remember, this fly is designed to be retrieved under the surface. The components of the fly and the method of fishing should go together.

That said, it can now be revealed that the fly will work equally well drifted deep. Tie it on a Duncan loop, leave about a six inch tag on the loop, form a ball of mono at the end of the tag by flicking a Bic at it, and attach the required number of split shot to the tag.

The discovery that a fly, tied as a flatwater emerger, also works well as a pocket water deep nymph was no great surprise; yet, when we fish it deep, it still goes by the name of Twitch-Pause Nymph. Why not? If flies can be named for their originators, rivers, materials, or the big naturals they represent, why not name them for the way they are fished, or for a memory? Thanks, John. Twitch-pause...

TWITCH-PAUSE NYMPH

HOOK:	Dai-Riki 070, Tiemco 3769 or equivalent, sizes 12-20
THREAD:	6/0 or 8/0 black or dark olive
BODY:	Crewel embroidery wool; comes in two ply, three strand twist, cut to length for tying and untwist, yields 3 pieces for 2 ply yarn; colors: lime green, dark olive, light tan, cinnamon brown
THROAT:	Mottled brown hen back feathers, lighter shades with lighter body, darker shades on darker bodies
HEAD:	Peacock herl

1. After wrapping the hook with tying thread select a single strand of the three strand crewel yarn.

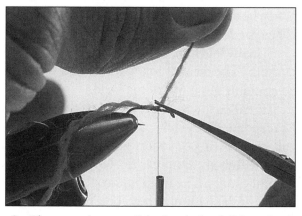

2. Tie on to the top of the hook the full length of the abdomen, this insures uniform proportions.

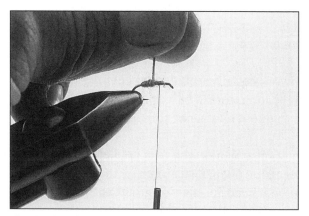

3. Twist the yarn with your fingers to rope and wrap a segmented body.

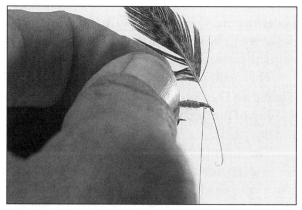

4. Select 6 to 8 fibers from a hen back feather for the throat.

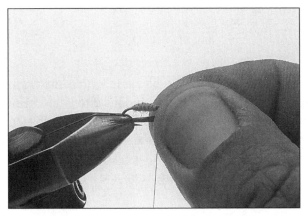

5. Tie in the throat fibers on the bottom of the hook. The length should be slightly past the bend of the hook.

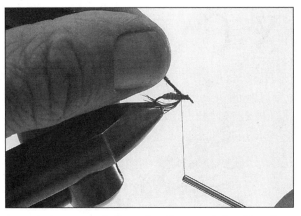

6. Tie in a couple strands of peacock herl by the butts as shown.

7. Wrap the peacock herl around the thread as shown.

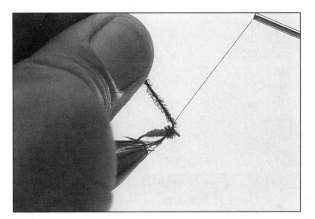

8. Make 2 to 3 wraps of peacock to form the head. Whip finish.

9. The finished Twitch-Pause Nymph.

X-CADDIS

Jay Buchner

My introduction to the X-Caddis came with a late night plea for a special fly. A guide friend and his client had been having tremendous success on a fly the client had purchased only a few of somewhere in Montana. They were down to the last fly and needed more ASAP because nothing else seemed to be working. By morning, they had a dozen to fish with and I had a few to try out.

A little research and I discovered that the X-Caddis was originated by Craig Mathews of Blue Ribbon Flies in West Yellowstone, Montana. It is an excellent caddis emerger pattern. The Z-lon tail represents an attached pupal shuck.

The X-Caddis works well even if there isn't an obvious caddis hatch in progress. Caddisflies often hatch sporadically, and although anglers may not be aware of their significance, the trout are looking for them. If you notice occasional hard splashy rise forms, you might want to try a X-Caddis.

X-CADDIS

HOOK:	Mustad 94845 or equivalent, sizes 12-16
THREAD:	6/0 or 8/0 olive or tan
TAIL:	Amber colored Z-lon
BODY:	Fine olive poly dubbing
WING:	Short fine body hair from mule deer, not whitetail deer

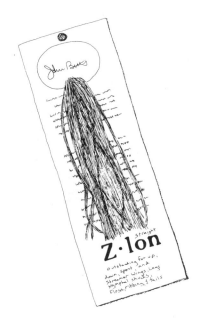

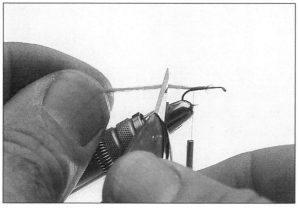

1. Secure the Z-lon tail and trim to length as shown.

2. Dub the thread.

3. Wrap a dubbed body on the rear 2/3 of the hook shank as shown.

4. Tie in short fine hair with the tips extending over the rear of the body. Trim the hair butts even and whip finish in front of them.

5. The finished X-Caddis.

P.T. EMERGER

Mike Lawson

You don't need a huge arsenal of patterns to match all of the mayflies you might encounter. I have adopted this philosophy after fishing Western spring creeks for so many years. I think that a great injustice is done to fly fishermen by those who stress the use of scientific names and a wide variety of patterns and colors to go with those names. The P.T. Emerger is my attempt to take a more generic approach toward fly selection.

In June of '91, I was giving a great deal of thought to the importance of mayfly emergers. On the Henry's Fork, this is the month when we get good hatches of Brown Drakes, Green Drakes, Pale Morning Duns, Blue Winged Olives and some Western Quills. The first thing I thought about was how many of these mayflies get trapped in their nymphal shucks during emergence and fall prey to the trout. Remember, I wanted to be generic. My guides and I all know that a Pheasant Tail Nymph is hard to beat when you know mayflies are around and active. I therefore used the back portion of the Pheasant Tail Nymph as the shuck portion of the P.T. Emerger.

For the emerging section of the fly, I wanted a material that would behave like a struggling mayfly emerger. I experimented with deer hair and duck quills, which worked, but not to my satisfaction. Since I had been trying to learn some things about CDC, it was a natural to try. It didn't do much to help the fly float, but it did trap air bubbles and gave the fly a soft movement in the water. Then I combined the CDC with Z-lon; it not only trapped air bubbles and moved, but it also scattered light. This gave the fly a real lifelike quality which was perfect.

It is my strong belief that a fly's primary features of behavior and shape (size and profile) outweigh color as a feature. There are four basic mayfly body colors: olive, yellow, tan and gray. Shades of these colors may vary for specific mayflies.

I have fished with the best of the best on the Henry's Fork, which is one of fly fishing's most famous and challenging waters. I'll tell you that all of these great anglers have their own personal favorite pattern for the identical hatch situation, and they all work because of a strong primary feature. That should tell you something.

In it's short existence, the P.T. Emerger has established itself as a deadly pattern in a variety of mayfly hatch situations. Simply adjust size and possibly color for different mayflies. I tie them as small as size 22 for Blue Winged Olives and as large as size 10 for Brown Drakes. Although there are quite a few steps needed to tie the P.T. Emerger, all of the steps are easy. It is a fly that I feature with confidence in both my catalog and fly shop.

PALE MORNING DUN P.T. EMERGER

HOOK:	Tiemco 100, Dai-Riki 305 or equivalent, sizes 10-22
THREAD:	8/0 brown or black Unithread
TAIL:	Rust colored Z-lon
BACK:	Rust colored Z-lon
ABDOMEN:	Pheasant tail feather fibers
RIBBING:	Fine reddish wire
THORAX:	Pale yellow very fine poly dubbing
UNDERWING:	Dun gray Z-lon
OVERWING:	2 tips of CDC feather, natural color or dun
LEGS:	Partridge body feather fibers
HEAD:	Same dubbing as thorax

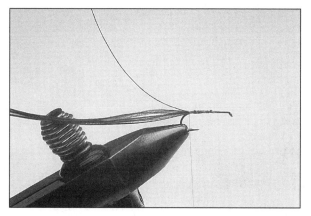

1. Tie in 6 to 8 pheasant tail feather fibers and the fine wire as shown.

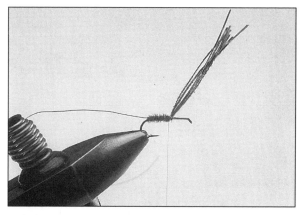

2. Wrap the pheasant tail fibers to mid hook shank.

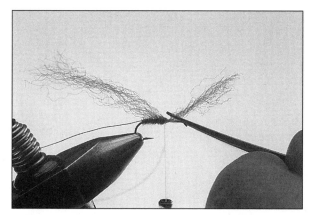

3. Attach Z-lon fibers over top of the hook shank and trim.

4. Pull the Z-lon over the back of the abdomen and secure with the wire ribbing.

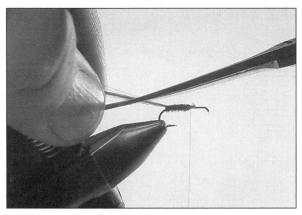

5. Pull Z-lon tail to stretch and cut at about 30 degree angle with the length about 3/4 of the hook.

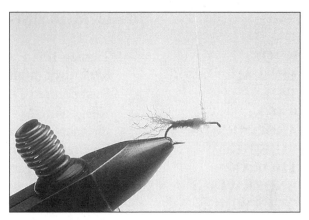

6. Dub a thorax.

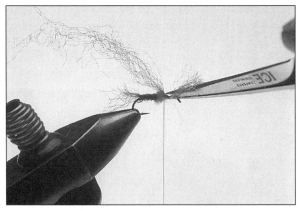

7. After attaching the Z-lon underwing to the top of the hook, trim the front stubs and cut the back at a 30 degree angle over the hook point.

8. Attach 2 CDC feather tips as an overwing the same length as the underwing. Can also use a clump of CDC fibers. Trim the butts.

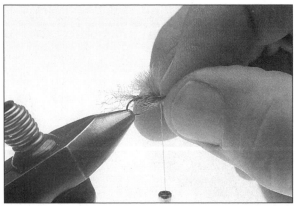

9. Tie in partridge feather fibers on the far side and near side as legs.

10. Secure all materials with head cement. Mike uses an old nail polish brush trimmed to a point to apply cement.

11. Dub the head. Whip finish.

12. Finished P.T. Emerger.

JAY'S HUMPBACK EMERGER

Jay Buchner

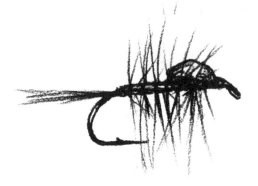

The idea for this fly came many years ago when I read Doug Swisher and Carl Richard's observations of stillborn insects in their book, *Fly Fishing Strategy*. In essence, they noted that the initial imitations they tied resembled Humpies and that..."the stillborn phenomenon may explain the effectiveness of these popular Western patterns, at least in smaller sizes."

Since I really like deer hair flies, I promptly tied some size 18 and 20 Humpies in Pale Morning Dun and Blue Wing Olive colors. The results were less than earth shaking. I caught an occasional trout, but there were many refusals between hookups. The idea still intrigued me, so the little Humpies stayed in my fly box. On those occasions when I would give them another shot at glory, the results continued to be inconsistent at best.

Finally, the idea behind Swisher and Richard's observations turned to an obsession with me. I examined one of the small Humpies and decided: the hump was too far back; there was too much hackle; and the tail material needed to be more translucent. Jay's Humpback Emerger is the result of adjustments to those perceived problems.

The first of these new emergers was tied in olive to fish a Blue Winged Olive Hatch. I field tested it on some very particular spring creek trout and I will assure you that refusals are no longer a problem. With the exception of adjusting colors, I have not modified the pattern.

JAY'S HUMPBACK EMERGER

HOOK:	Mustad 94845 or equivalent, sizes 14-22
THREAD:	6/0 or 8/0 olive or color of natural
TAIL:	Brown hackle fibers
BODY:	Thread or fine dubbing, color of natural
HACKLE:	Dun or dun dyed grizzly neck hackle
BACK:	Deer body hair

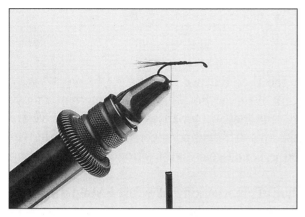

1. Attach a hackle fiber tail as shown.

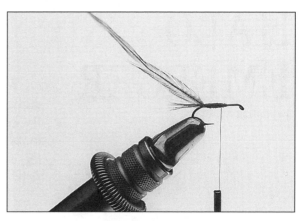

2. Tie in hackle feather at the rear.

3. Tie in cleaned, stacked hair at mid shank. Length is not important. The body should be covered with either thread or dubbing at this point.

4. Palmer hackle to just behind the eye.

5. Pull the hair over to create a hump as shown. Trim the hair tips. Whip finish the head.

6. Finished Jay's Humpback Emerger.

HALO EMERGER

Gary LaFontaine

Why are the flies that we develop so different? Why don't they look like everybody else's perception of a mayfly, caddisfly or stonefly? Our answer to that is that we are looking at it from a different perspective. We are underwater, bedecked in scuba gear and positioned below moving fish.

The method of observation that we use is simple trial and error. The fly passes over and the fish either responds or doesn't respond. It is the fish giving us the answers, not humans. So, as a result, we don't care what a fly looks like. We don't care how wild and strange it is. We just keep testing different parts of it until the trout tells us what he wants to see. It is not the perspective of a human; it is the perspective of a fish. And yes, that often ends up being very different.

Now, let's look at the Halo Emerger. Is it a perfect imitation? No. The last thing an angler wants on a trout stream is a perfect imitation. If there is a heavy hatch and there are thirty-five mayflies going past a trout's nose every minute, the perfect imitation is going to be the thirty-sixth fly going by his nose. An angler doesn't need the perfect imitation, he needs a fly that is better than perfect. How can a fly be better than perfect? By exaggerating the primary characteristic. If that characteristic is prominent enough, the trout will select the artificial fly over the natural.

The Halo Emerger qualifies as a super pattern. It is a fly that the angler can put on during a heavy hatch when the fish are feeding selectively and feel confident that he is going to do much better than normal, simply because the fly will work better than a perfect imitation.

This pattern looks like a mayfly just popping its wings, floating down a stream and struggling in the surface film. During that process with the natural insect, an escape hole splits on the top of the nymph's thorax and the wings begin to unfold. An aura of light spreads over the insect, along the edges of that escape hole. Closed cell foam recreates this aura, or halo of light, on the Halo Emerger.

The foam flairs out around the thorax. Trout choose the exaggerated aura of the fly over the natural brightness of an insect. When a heavy hatch begins, and the fish get fussy, the Halo Emerger becomes an indispensable pattern.

HALO EMERGER

HOOK:	Dai-Riki 300 or equivalent, sizes 8-24
THREAD:	8/0, color to match
TAG:	Clear Antron wrapped down the bend of the hook
TAIL:	Marabou fibers to match the body color
WING:	Closed cell foam
BODY:	Fine poly dubbing, color of natural
FORWARD WING:	Always orange dyed elk or deer hair

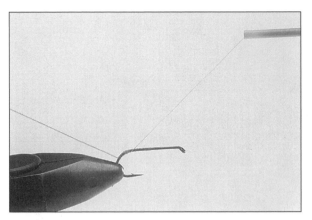

1. Tie in a piece of clear Antron at the rear of the hook.

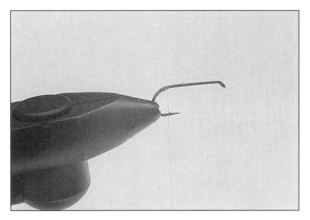

2. Wrap a tag with the clear Antron down the bend of the hook as shown.

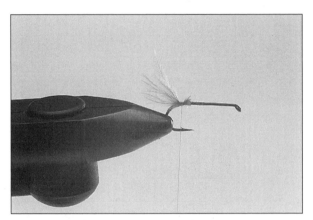

3. Tie in marabou fibers for the tail.

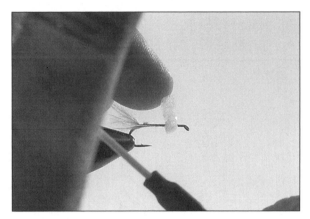

4. Secure closed cell foam 1/3 back from the eye by ' X-ing ' the thread, then fold each side up and secure with individual thread wraps (forms envelope).

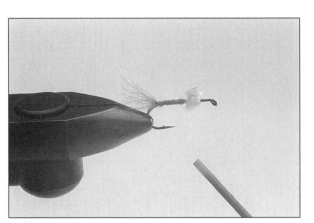

5. Dub a slight abdomen.

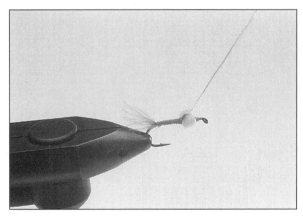

6. Form a thorax by figure eighting through the foam wing.

7. Tie in forewing of elk or deer hair. Trim and whip finish.

8. The finished Halo Emerger.

Gary LaFontaine

The Mess is another one of our very strange looking patterns utilizing closed cell foam. When most people look at it they do so with great skepticism. The Mess imitates large mayfly adults struggling to free themselves from the water. These insects are some of the hardest to imitate because of their size. Most of the fly patterns developed to imitate these large insects are (this is a strong opinion) mediocre at best.

One time in Pennsylvania, Greg Hoover, who is a fine writer and entomologist, came up and told me:

"I was at Rusty Gate's shop on the Ausable in Michigan and there were some people there who had read *The Dry Fly*. They felt the theory behind the Mess was wrong. One man said flatly, 'Look at this fly. It's supposed to imitate a large mayfly. We have a lot of patterns for this river, developed over the years for the Hex hatch, and this thing doesn't look like any of them. It will never work.' Well, someone tied some up, gave them to him, and told him to go out and see what happened. He disappeared out the door with a few of the Mess and little faith. Hours later he returned wide-eyed, 'I have never had a night on the Hex hatch like this one.'"

That is what happens with this pattern. It takes a while to break down the skepticism. Once an angler gives it a fair test, he develops faith in it. It's not the oddity of the Mess that makes it good, but the fact that there are certain characteristics that are so exaggerated that the trout are fascinated by the fly. The Mess is worth trying anytime big mayflies, size 12 or larger, are hatching.

MESS

HOOK:	Dai-Riki 300 or equivalent, sizes 8-12
THREAD:	8/0 color to match body
TAIL:	4 dun hackle fibers
BACK:	Closed cell foam strip cut wide
UNDERBODY:	Scintilla #53 Crawdaddy or orange sparkle blend
HACKLE:	One dun neck feather or one mallard flank feather

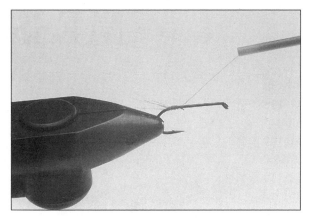

1. Tie in and flare 4 hackle fibers for a tail.

2. Tie in closed cell foam strip as shown.

3. Dub the body 2/3 forward as shown.

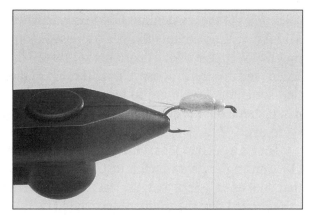

4. Pull the foam over to form a back. Tie off and trim.

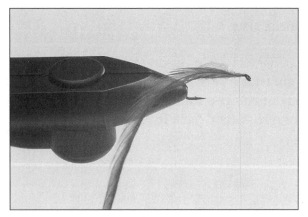

5. Tie in a neck hackle on the near side of the hook.

6. Make 2 to 3 wraps of hackle. Tie off and trim.

7. Tie in the mallard flank feather and make 1 to 2 turns in front of the other hackle.

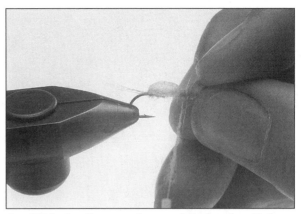

8. With the fingers of your right hand pull the hackle fibers forward over the eye of the hook and dub behind them forcing the hackle to point forward. Whip finish.

9. The finished Mess.

Aquatic Adult Insects

CALLIBAETIS CUT-WING MAYFLY

Pat Berry

The concept of a cut-wing fly is certainly not new, but it's a fresh enough approach so that many variations are still possible. A cut-wing itself is an easy way to attain some of the more exacting qualities that a fly may need to work well over fussy fish. The wings give a realistic silhouette that many anglers feel are important from a fish's point of view.

I have spent a lot of time observing the natural insects on the water trying to decide the best way to imitate my perspective on how mayflies actually pose while at rest. First of all, the wings don't sit forward or even completely vertical as some patterns suggest. Instead the wings are cocked back towards the tail at an angle. Some upright winged spinners even have the back edge of their wings nearly touching the top of their abdomen. Secondly, the bodies of mayflies often curl up at the tail suggesting a bend in the abdomen. Most bodies on mayfly imitations are limited to the straight quality of the hook shank. Lastly, most imitations wrap the hackle evenly on either side of the wing. When a mayfly sits at rest on the water, only it's two small hind legs actually extend behind the wing. The insect's larger forelegs usually sit to the side or the front of the thorax and wing.

The pattern that I concocted--with a lot of help from Ken Iwamasa's tying ideas and Gary LaFontaine's concepts on dry flies--corrects some of the preconceived notions of how mayflies should be imitated. I usually save this fly for very tough fish that need to see something that looks as close to the real thing as possible. And it is really not that tough to tie.

The pattern was first experimented with by Jeff Currier on the Henry's Fork. I tied some that he could use during the impressive *E. flavilinea* hatches that the Henry's Fork sees. The fish over at Last Chance and in the Ranch area see a number of anglers every year, and consequently a lot of different patterns. Some of the larger fish need to see a more exact imitation of the natural, and because you may only get a few casts over each fish, you need a fly that will consistently land correctly. The "Flav" imitation lands perfectly and fools even the pickiest fish consistently.

Exceptional feedback came from a fellow who stopped in Jack Dennis' Shop one day. I showed him this new pattern just so he could see how other flies should be cut straight across the bottom of the hackle. He was very interested in trying my fly and attempting to tie some of his own copies. After much pressure and prodding, I finally gave him one and told him his payment to me would be some sort of feedback in the future. Sure enough, the gentleman returned a few weeks later with a huge grin on his face. The fly landed right, floated great, and fooled even the toughest fish!

My own experience has met with the same success. It especially amazed me one day when I fished a hatch in Yellowstone Park. The fish were obviously taking emergers but I snatched the old cut-wing out of my box anyway. I'll be damned if it didn't work incredibly well. Maybe the fish mistook it for an emerger because the body sits so low in the water.

It's extremely important to cut the hackle correctly so that the fly floats properly on the water. If it is tied correctly, it acts like a cat and almost always lands on its feet.

120

CUT WING CALLIBAETIS

HOOK:	Tiemco 100, Dai-Riki 305 or equivalent, sizes 10-18
THREAD:	6/0 black
UNDERBODY:	Very fine poly dubbing, Adams gray color
TAIL:	5-6 strands moose body hair
OVERBODY:	Elk hair, natural dark or deer hair
WINGS:	Cut grizzly hen saddle hackle
THORAX:	Same as underbody
HACKLE:	Grizzly hackle

NOTE: Sizes and colors can be varied to match everything from a size 10 Green Drake to a size 18 Pale Morning Dun

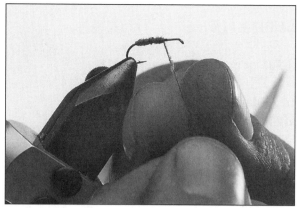

1. Dub a slim body from above the hook point to about 1/3 back from the eye.

2. Tie in moose hair as shown 1 1/2 hook shank lengths.

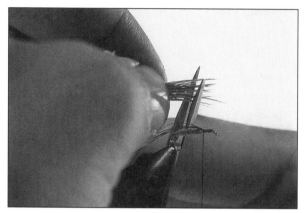

3. Select out a small bunch of elk hair. Trim the tips.

4. Tie in with the trimmed tips forward where the dubbing ends. The length of the hair doesn't matter because it will be trimmed.

5. Wrap the thread back to rib the body as shown.

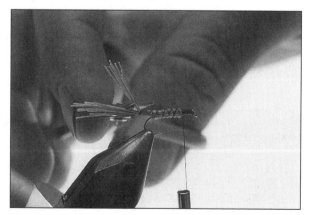

6. After reverse ribbing with the thread trim the butts of the elk hair as shown.

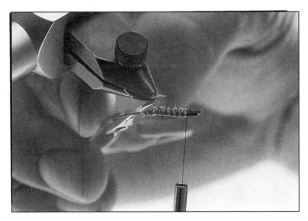

7. Be sure in trimming to leave the moose hair tail.

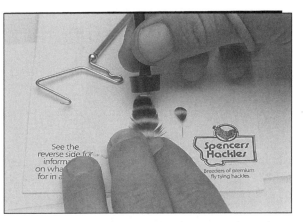

8. Cut the hen saddle with the appropriate size wing cutter as shown. A cardboard backing will help in cutting.

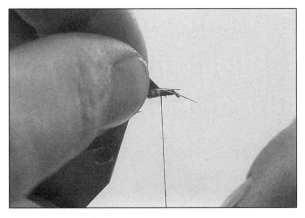

9. Tie in the wings with the stems on the top of the hook. The curves should face each other to form a single wing.

10. Secured wing, note that it is angled slightly back. Wing base can be glued here.

11. Select the appropriate size grizzly hackle.

12. Tie in the hackle at the far side of the hook in front of the wing and dub the thorax as shown.

13. Wrap the hackle through the dubbed thorax and whip finish.

14. Trim the hackle on the bottom of the fly.

15. Glue the head and the base of the tail.

16. Finished Cut-Wing Callibaetis

PARACHUTE HARE'S EAR

Jack Dennis

The Parachute Hare's Ear is the creation of Californian, Ed Schroeder. Paul Bruun, a Jackson Hole fishing guide and outdoor sports writer became a big fan of Ed's pattern in '88, after being introduced to the fly by another area guide, Bryan Tarantola.

Paul searched Ed out at a '89 winter sports show to get some background material on the Parachute Hare's Ear for his newspaper column. He reported that Ed originated the Parachute Hare's Ear in the early 70's while guiding on California's Kings River. Ed explained:

"Below one of the dams on the Kings River near Merced the water was so cold that during massive caddis fly hatches, the emerging insects were frozen on the way to the surface. We would see mats of these caddis floating past, and the big fish would concentrate on them because the eating was so easy. But this created several problems. First, it was wholly impossible to see your fly amid all the naturals and often the fish were actually taking flies riding higher than the greased Hare's Ear nymphs I began fishing."

Although the Parachute Hare's Ear may have it's origins as a frozen caddis imitation, it's true niche is as a generic mayfly imitation. Tied in sizes 14 through 22, it will perform well during hatches ranging from *Callibaetis* to *Tricos*. Many fly fishermen prefer the parachute tie because it can be taken by the trout as either a dun, cripple or spinner. No one will argue that it is easy to see with it's upwing.

Hare's ear is not the only material that can be used to dub the body of this parachute style of fly. Materials and colors can be substituted. Calf body hair is the first choice for the wing, but suitable substitutes are poly yarn and even Krystal Flash (good on little *Tricos*). Both of these substitute wing materials are inexpensive and easy to work with.

In the tying instructions that follow, Scott Sanchez' technique for splitting the tail of the fly will be used. Scott's technique also bombproofs the hackle and wing.

By the way, Paul Bruun reports that he can still catch anything with spots on it in the Snake River using a Parachute Hare's Ear. That's no small statement coming from a man of Paul's stature.

PARACHUTE HARE'S EAR

HOOK:	Dai-Riki 305 or equivalent, sizes 14-22
THREAD:	8/0 brown
WING:	White calf body hair, or white calf tail
TAIL:	Elk mane
BODY:	Hare's ear dubbing
RIBBING:	8/0 brown thread from dubbing loop
HACKLE BRACE:	8/0 brown thread from dubbing loop
HACKLE:	Grizzly neck hackle

1. Tie in a small bunch of stacked calf body hair at the halfway point with the tips forward as shown.

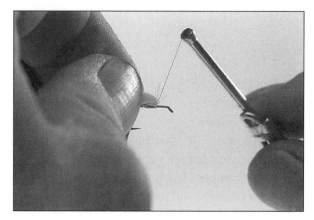

2. Pull the tips back and make numerous thread wraps to stand the wing upright.

3. Make wraps around the wing to bunch it together in a post.

4. Tie in the hackle, shiny side up (curve down) on the near side of the hook and behind the wing.

5. Form a loop with the thread at the bend of the hook. This will be used to split the tail and rib the body.

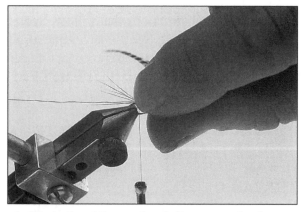

6. Tie in 8 to 10 strands of elk mane or hock as a tail. Length should be the same as the shank. Press down with the index fingernail to flare.

7. Pull the thread loop through the middle of the flared tail which will split them and secure the loop with the thread. Don't cut the loop.

8. Dub a tapered body forward to the base of the wing and rib with the loop. Don't cut the loop either. Make sure it's tied off on top of the hook shank.

9. Continue the dubbing to just behind the head.

10. Wrap the hackle around the wing post in a counter clockwise direction 4 to 8 wraps depending on fly size.

11. Tie off the hackle with thread at the front as shown.

12. Pull the thread loop through the wing. This will keep the hackle from sliding up the wing post and coming off.

13. Tie off the loop, trim and whip finish.

14. Finished Parachute Hare's Ear.

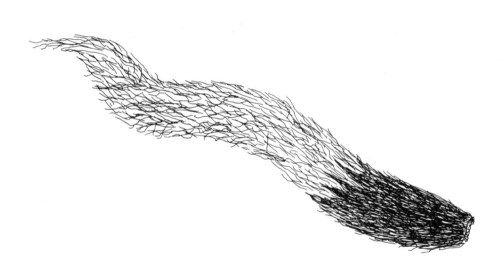

LOOP WING ADAMS

Jack Dennis

Loop wing mayfly patterns were introduced by an innovative fly tier named Andre Puyans. As it is with so many things that are different, the loop wing style has its adversaries and advocates. Some anglers complain that the air resistance created by the loop wing causes the fly to spin when cast. An advocate might argue that this is a function of leader length, casting technique or a good excuse for not catching fish.

The wing on the earlier loop wings was formed from the fibers of flank feathers from mallard, partridge and pheasant. The loops can be divided and secured by a figure eight tying procedure.

Chuck Stranahan remembers that Bob Quigley went a step further with the loop wing design. "Bob took Andre's idea and created the popular Loop Wing Paraduns and Loop Wing Spinners. He used everything from clipped hackle stems to waxed elk hair to form loops."

After mentioning the above options, we are going to use a completely different material for the loop wing. Scott Sanchez has a great imagination when it comes to tying flies. He tied loop wings using both Krystal Flash and Flashabou. The Krystal Flash twists when the loop is tied down, giving an interesting silhouette of the wing. The Flashabou forms a near perfect wing. Both materials scatter light very well and are extremely durable.

The loop wing style is a viable option for a mayfly wing on patterns you tie. Give it a try when tying Adams or other mayfly imitations. You might be particularly surprised and pleased with the results you get using Flashabou.

LOOP WING ADAMS

HOOK:	Dai-Riki 305 or equivalent, sizes 10-22
THREAD:	8/0 iron gray
TAIL:	Gray Microfibetts
WING:	Pearl Flashabou
BODY:	Adams gray very fine poly dubbing
HACKLE:	Grizzly neck hackle

1. Use the same thread loop technique to split the tail as in the Parachute Hare's Ear, page 126-127 steps 5-7.

2. Note the split tail and the thread loop secured forward of the split tail.

3. Dub a slight tapered body forward as shown and rib with the thread loop. Tie off and trim the loop.

4. Tie in several strands of pearl Flashabou on top of the hook and the hackle on the near side of the hook. The dull side of the hackle should face you.

5. Dub a thorax.

6. Wrap the hackle through the thorax as shown.

7. Trim the hackle flush to the thorax on the bottom of the hook.

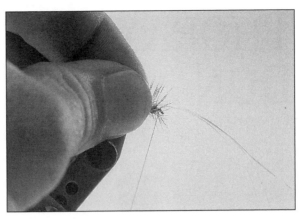

8. Pull the Flashabou forward and tie down with a couple of loose wraps of thread. Do not trim the Flashabou at this point.

9. Work the scissor tips underneath the Flashabou and pull up to the desired wing height. Trim and whip finish.

10. Finished Loop-Winged Adams.

NOTE: You can easily change this pattern to an emerger by: 1) Replacing the split tail with a chopped hackle fiber tail as used in the Barr Emerger. 2) By pulling the Flashabou to a shorter height simulating a splitting wing case.

THORAX DUN

Mike Lawson

By no means was I the first to tie the Thorax Dun. Credit for this pattern goes to the late Vince Marinaro, whose thorax tie had crisscrossed hackle of two different sizes. I first saw a generalized thorax pattern in an Orvis catalog, so it had been around awhile when I started tying it.

The way I tie the Thorax Dun is really not a modification of Marinaro's style, but more of a modification of a parachute style mayfly. The parachute tie sits down in the water, which isn't what the natural duns do. The natural mayfly sits up on the water with its legs dimpling the surface. By cutting a 'V' in the hackle, my variation of the Thorax Dun is stable on the water so it won't roll on it's side, and it does a good job of mimicking the dimpling of the natural. My way of tying it is also much simpler than crisscrossing two hackles as Marinaro did. I never could tie those worth a darn.

I usually tie the Thorax Dun to imitate mayflies no larger than a size 14. I prefer turkey flat feathers for the post wing, but other materials will work; try Z-lon, poly yarn or bird feathers such as partridge. This is probably one place where CDC feathers do not have a practical application. To be effective, CDC should come in contact with the water where it can trap air bubbles and also move. Those things won't happen with a post wing. When tying the post wing, it is important that it's height be the same as the body is long.

I prefer the Thorax Dun to other mayfly patterns for spring creek fishing. It has a very good response when trout are on the feed for a specific hatch of small mayflies.

When I used to guide more than I do now, it was frustrating to get out on the Henry's Fork in the morning with clients and see all those fish working but not be able to catch any. In the early morning here, the trout get extremely selective on spent mayfly spinners. What I learned to do was to clip the post wing down on the Thorax Dun to imitate the spents. The clients, who would otherwise be doing nothing but grinding their teeth in disgust, would do real well with this technique. You know, I still use this technique today.

In his book, *The Dry Fly New Angles*, Gary LaFontaine has some great observations on the Thorax Dun. I would strongly recommend his work as a reference. A couple of his comments do a good job of summing up my feelings about this fly:

"In the slower flow, where trout settled under a fly and stared at it as they rose, the Thorax Dun got fewer late refusals than any other type mayfly imitation...The Thorax Duns are valuable as more than just spring creek flies because there are micro-habitats, little pieces of any river, where trout study secondary characteristics of an imitation...drifts will have to be very precise, the pattern entering the window exactly where the trout looks for the next mayfly, and they'll have to be timed to the trout's rise rhythm. Still, once he gets the fish to look at the fly, the battle will be fairly won."

PALE MORNING DUN THORAX

HOOK:	Tiemco 100, Dai-Riki 305 or equivalent, sizes 12-22
THREAD:	6/0 or 8/0 pale yellow
TAIL:	Dun hackle fibers
BODY:	Pale yellow fine poly dubbing
WING:	Med. dun turkey flat
HACKLE:	Dun neck hackle

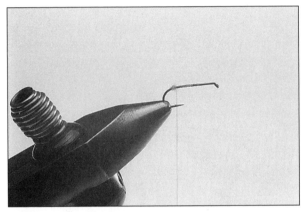

1. Make a small ball of dubbing on the hook shank above the barb.

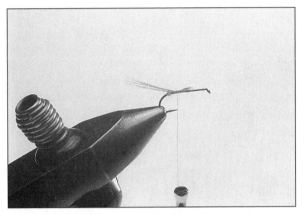

2. Tie in a small group of dun hackle fibers in front of the dubbing ball but not tight to the ball.

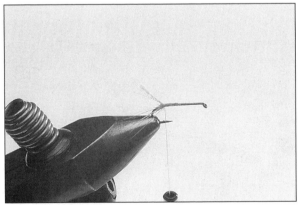

3. While wrapping the thread back to the ball, split the tail equally to each side of the ball with your fingers. The finished split tail as shown.

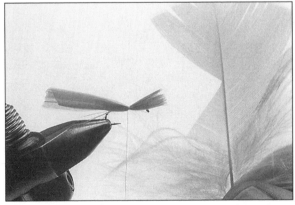

4. Attach the wing material at mid-shank with tips forward.

5. Stand the wing up with thread wraps and trim the butts. Note the length of the wing.

6. Attach the dun hackle with the stem on the near side with the dull side facing you.

7. Dub the entire body from tail to head with taper as shown.

8. Wrap the hackle to the front three wraps behind and three wraps in front of the wing. Trim and whip finish.

9. Cut the bottom of the hackle in a 'V'.

10. Finished Thorax Dun.

NO-HACKLE

by Mike Lawson

One day a group of guys came into the shop on their way back from fishing Nelson's Spring Creek in Livingston, Montana. One fellow in the group was a big fan of the No-Hackle, while the others had been non-believers. They had bet on who could catch the most fish on Nelson's with a single fly of their choice. The No-Hackle guy caught around 30 and was the winner by a big margin. That should tell you something.

A lot of people knock the durability of the duck quill wings on the No-Hackle. The wings do separate after a few fish chew them, and they can even come apart from false casting, but that doesn't diminish their effectiveness. Duck quill wings may fray, but they don't tear. Put a duck quill between your thumbnail and fingernail and try to tear it. I have tried every type of natural and synthetic material over the years and not one of them has the strength of duck quill. It is important, however, to use some kind of silicone crystals to get slime off the fly between fish.

There are references to No-Hackle style flies from the last century. But, it is Doug Swisher and Carl Richards who should get credit for the fly as we know it today. After the arrival of their classic book, *Selective Trout,* the No-Hackle became very popular and consequently René Harrop (a well-known fly tier) was swamped with orders for them. He asked if I would help him out by tying some and showed me how they were tied. After working on some big orders, I got pretty polished on how to do it.

The No-Hackle is probably more of an emerger than a dun because of where it floats in the surface film. Although it works as large as a size 12, I feel that in 16 to 24 it will outperform any other mayfly pattern.

I think that Doug Swisher and Carl Richards' entire series of flies are the most innovative patterns to arrive on the fly tying scene for a long time. They recognized the importance of emerging insects to selectively feeding trout and deserve a lot of credit for their contributions to fly tying. I'll tell you, their No-Hackle is definitely one of my favorite patterns.

PALE MORNING DUN NO-HACKLE

HOOK:	Tiemco 100, Dai-Riki 305 or equivalent, sizes 14-22
THREAD:	6/0 or 8/0 pale yellow
TAIL:	Dun hackle fibers
BODY:	Pale yellow fine poly
WING:	Sections from a right & left wing feather from a mallard duck

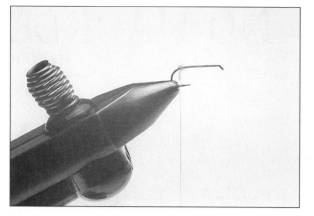

1. Dub a small ball at the butt as shown.

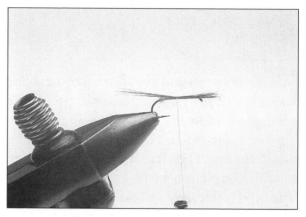

2. Attach dun hackle fibers for the tail. Fibers should extend a hook shank length beyond the dubbed ball.

3. Use a few wraps of thread at a time to flare the fibers and then divide them with your fingers to give right and left outriggers as shown.

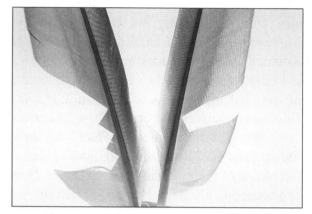

4. Cut a right and left wing from a right and left mallard duck wing feather. The width of the wing should be 1/2 as long as the hook shank.

5. Use your thumb and index finger to pinch the quills in place. Note, the wing height should be the same as the length of the body.

6. Pull the thread back in the same plane as the hook shank. Use fingers of the left hand when winging. (note hackle pliers are used in the next steps for clarity only) Page 138, Illustration A.

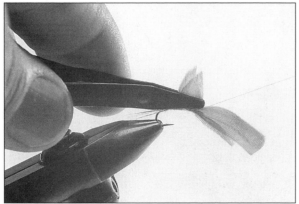

7. Bring the thread forward near the side of the wing and drop over the eye of the hook. Page 138, illustration B.

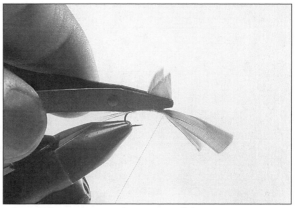

8. Make one complete turn of thread around the hook shank. Page 138, illustration B.

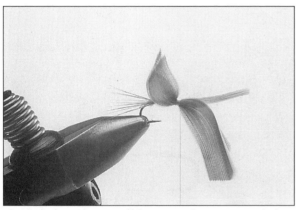

9. It is just not possible to see how to stand the wings up because your fingers are in the way. See the illustration of how the thread is pulled straight back and up at a 45 degree angle. Page 138, illustration C.

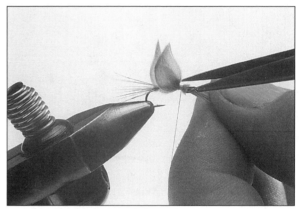

10. Trim the butts of the quill wings as shown.

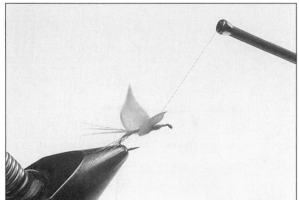

11. Figure eight the thread to separate the wings. Page 138, Illustration D.

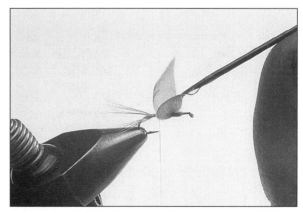

12. Put a small drop of Flexament in the seam between the wings. Do not stick the wings together or add weight to the fly with a big drop.

13. Dub the body as far up into the wings as possible, do not figure eight between the wings. Dub to the eye of the hook.

14. Finished No-Hackle.

A.

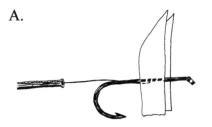

B.

C.

Correct direction of thread.

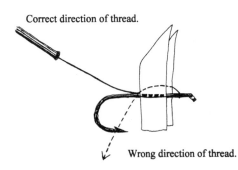

Wrong direction of thread.

D.

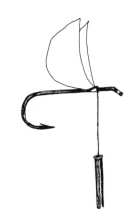

COMPARADUN

Jack Dennis

Both the Comparadun and Sparkle Dun evolved from an older fly pattern called the Haystack, which was developed by Francis Betters, creator of the famous Ausable Wulff.

In his fine book, *Mastering the Art of Fly Tying*, Dick Talleur gives an interesting background on the Haystack. He notes that Betters found the Haystack suitable as an emerger if it was twitched under the surface; a mayfly dun with it's upright profile when fished dry; or as a caddis if twitched dry during caddis activity. That is not a bad cross-section of trout food!

The Comparadun was developed by Al Caucci. It replaces the deer hair tail of the Haystack with a tail of divided hackle fibers. The divided or split tail gives a realistic impression of the south end of a mayfly dun and also acts as an outrigger to stabilize the fly on the water. The deer hair wing of the Haystack is somewhat upright, while the Comparadun wing is flared in a 180 degree arc.

The Sparkle Dun comes from Craig Mathews and John Juracek of Blue Ribbon Flies in West Yellowstone, Montana. The flared wing remains the same as the Comparadun wing, but the tail is comprised of Z-lon or sparkle yarn. This material represents a nymphal shuck and gives the fly the appearance of a stillborn or cripple mayfly, whose tail and/or legs have not escaped the shuck. A trout will refuse some natural duns, but rarely allow a cripple or stillborn to drift past its window.

One key in tying these flies, as with any hair fly, is to select the proper piece of deer hair, in this case for the wing. It should be short on the hide and hollow. Look for natural mule deer hair that is light shaded (light gray) through the length of the hair, not dark. Short coarse hair flares well and the hollowness enhances flotation. Fine hair will neither flare nor float well.

Both the Comparadun and Sparkle Dun do a great job of imitating small mayflies. They are durable and simple to tie. Remember, you are only dealing with the basic insect anatomy here (tail, body and wing). Simply adjust size and body color to match the hatch.

PALE MORNING DUN COMPARADUN

HOOK:	Mustad 94845 or equivalent, sizes 14-22
THREAD:	6/0 pale yellow
TAIL:	White Microfibett
BODY:	Fine pale yellow poly dubbing
WING:	Deer shoulder hair
SPECIAL:	Dave's Flexament for front and rear wing base

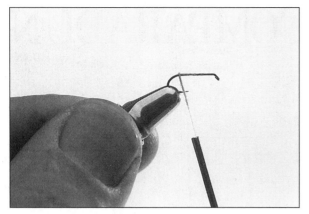

1. Dub a ball on the hook shank above the barb.

2. Select out a small bunch of Microfibetts. Using a wire tester makes this easier.

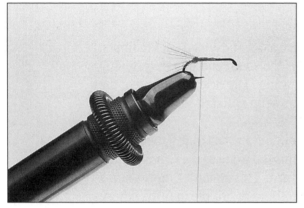

3. Split the Microfibett tail in the same fashion as was used to split the hackle fiber tail in the Thorax Dun, page 133, steps 2,3.

4. Tie the hair in at mid shank with loose wraps making progressively tighter wraps toward the front to flare the wing 180 degrees.

5. Trim the hair butts. Make thread wraps in front of the wing to stand it up then wrap the thread over the trimmed butts. Secure with an application of Dave's Flexament.

6. Begin dubbing in front of the ball.

7. Dub a tapered body forward to the eye and whip finish.

8. Side and forward views of the finished Comparadun.

Wire Tester Type Hackle Pliers

CHUCK'S STONEFLIES

Chuck Stranahan

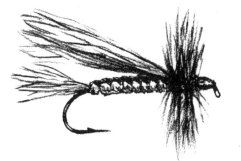

Northern California's fabled Hat Creek offers a number of unique opportunities to anglers; among them, the prospect of fishing abundant Salmonfly and Golden Stone hatches on flat, spring creek water.

These fish will take Salmonflies and Goldens as deliberately as they do Pale Morning Duns, providing you use proper presentation and realistic fly design. Over the years, I have found that flies seem to work best when they have a silhouette which mimics the natural as seen from underneath, especially with respects to the wing. Ideally, this part of the anatomy should be sparse, so as to simulate the venation and motion of the natural, not the opaque "shaving brush" of many of our western patterns.

Bodies seem to work best when they are flattened, segmented, darkened on the sides so as not to reflect light, and tied to rest half-submerged in the surface film. And finally, I've noticed repeatedly that the splat of an abdomen-first descent which makes about the same commotion on the surface as a natural, is a triggering factor which produces many strikes. In fact, I've seen fish put down by the dive of bullet head artificials.

Cal Bird designed his famous, prototypical Bird's Stone pattern for Hat Creek years ago. The splat of its descent was a factor in Cal's fly. I've tried to pay attention to the splat and wing silhouette of the fly as Cal did, while modifying the body.

The elk hair underbody and acrylic yarn combination produces a segmented and oval shaped body which floats low in the surface film but is buoyant, particularly when dressed with some of the modern liquid floatants.

While most of my informal, trial-and-error research was focused on the Salmonfly, the Golden is, on many streams, more significant. After working out the Salmonfly, all I needed to do was change the color and size for the Golden Stone.

Goldens provide the angler with opportunities on many of our rivers which are not sufficiently recognized. Water is generally lower and clearer when Goldens occur. It doesn't take a ton of bugs to have the fish key on them. As on Hat Creek, fantastic fishing can be found during the late evenings when egg-laying Goldens dive bomb the riffles, and any big yellow fly will work. The same fish, when keyed to Goldens, will often take a sparse winged, low riding imitation as a searching pattern during the middle of the day. Fishing such a fly any time Goldens are present, or even a week after they have disappeared, might provide some pleasant surprises for anglers who are accustomed to searching the water with attractors.

CHUCK'S SALMONFLY

HOOK:	Tiemco 5212, 5263, Dai-Riki 710 or equivalent, sizes 4-8
THREAD:	3/0 fluorescent flame red
TAIL:	Orange dyed elk hair, coarse flank hair preferred
UNDERBODY:	Same as tail
BODY:	Red Heart brand 100% acrylic 4-ply yarn, pumpkin color or similar; mark the top & sides with a brown permanent felt marker
WING:	Moose hair; straight, fine texture body or shoulder works best
OVERWING:	White calf tail as in Riverbend Olive Stone, page 149, steps 11&12
HACKLE:	2 Spencer brown dyed grizzly saddle hackles, one golden ginger dyed grizzly hackles; can substitute grizzly and other colored feathers to get a multishaded effect

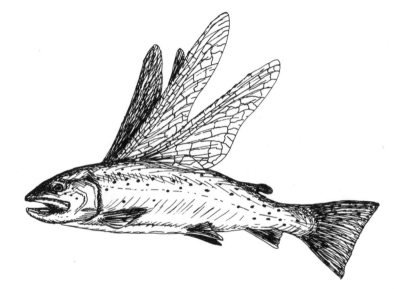

CHUCK'S GOLDEN STONE

HOOK:	Tiemco 5212 or equivalent, sizes 6-10
THREAD:	3/0 tan or golden olive monocord
TAIL:	Natural elk hair
UNDERBODY:	Same as tail
BODY:	Red Heart brand 100% acrylic 4-ply yarn, old gold color or similar; shade top and sides of body with a brown permanent felt marker
WING:	Natural elk hair, fine shoulder or mane preferred
HACKLE:	2 Spencer golden ginger dyed grizzly saddle hackles

NOTE: Wing and hackle shades should blend together rather than contrast. Adjust to specific hatches with lighter or darker shades.

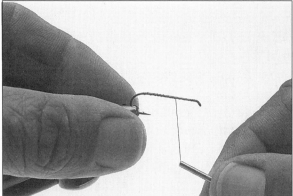

1. Wrap a base of thread from the eye of the hook to the bend then 2/3 back up the hook shank.

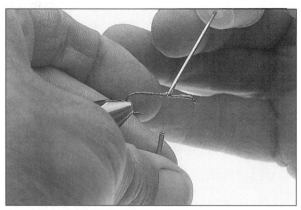

2. Cement the thread base just before step 3.

3. After selecting the tail/underbody hair, stack and measure for length. Tail extends beyond the bend of the hook 1/3 shank length.

4. Secure the hair bundle about 1/3 shank length back from the eye with several wraps keeping the hair on top of the hook shank.

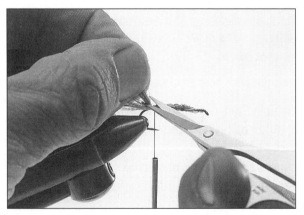

5. Grasp excess tail hair and trim out as shown. This will keep the tail slight and yet allow a bulky stonefly body.

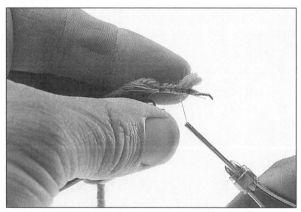

6. Tie in the yarn as shown and cover the tips with thread forming an evenly proportioned underbody.

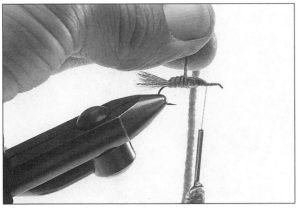

7. After sealing the underbody with head cement, rope a segmented body as shown by twisting the yarn.

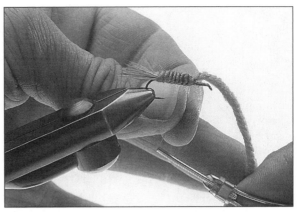

8. While keeping the yarn twisted, secure with thread at the position shown.

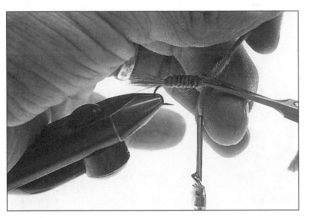

9. Trim the yarn at an angle and cover tapered ends with thread.

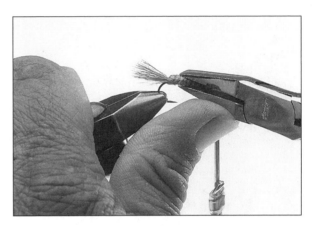

10. Flatten the body with smooth jawed pliers. The body should be wider than it is thick.

11. Color the top and each side of the body with the felt tip marker using a single stroke on each surface.

12. Select the hair for the wing; trim and stack. The wing length should not extend beyond the tail.

13. Tie in the wing with tight wraps in the front making looser wraps toward the rear. The hair is flared by pressing down with the thumbnail as shown then securing with tight wraps.

14. Cement the wing base as shown. When viewed from the side the sparse wing only flares a few degrees and its sparseness from below simulates a fluttering wing.

15. Select 2 saddle hackles for proper size.

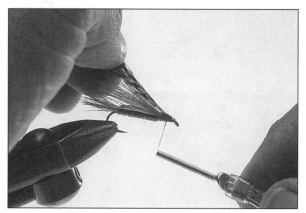

16. Tie in hackles on top of the wing base with the dull side forward.

17. Cement a foundation before wrapping the hackle. Wrap the hackle forward, trim and whip finish.

18. The finished Chuck's Golden Stone.

RIVERBEND OLIVE STONE

Chuck Stranahan

The Riverbend Stone series is typified by the olive, or *Skwala* stonefly shown here. Tied for the pre-runoff olive stonefly hatch which provides some of the best activity on the Bitterroot River, the Riverbend Olive sits low in the water, has a distinct body silhouette, and, with the white overwing, offers plenty of visibility for the angler despite the fly's low profile and dark color.

This style fills the bill wherever a spent stonefly is called for (from salmonflies to the *Claassenia* stoneflies of the Snake River, to the Little Yellow Sallies which are abundant throughout the West). Change materials and hook size as required. The basic dressing here works in sizes 6 through 16.

Finally, clip the hackle on the bottom. This will help the fly to land upright and float flush in the surface film. As my maturity advances (as evidenced by the lines across my face), I appreciate these subtleties more each season.

RIVERBEND OLIVE STONE

HOOK:	Tiemco 5212 or equivalent, sizes 6-10
THREAD:	3/0 olive monocord
TAIL:	Olive dyed elk hair; coarse hollow flank hair preferred
UNDERBODY:	Same as tail
BODY:	Brown/olive dubbing
HEAD:	Brown dyed elk; fine textured mane or shoulder preferred
UNDERWING:	Same as head
OVERWING:	White calf tail
HACKLE:	Olive dyed grizzly saddle hackle

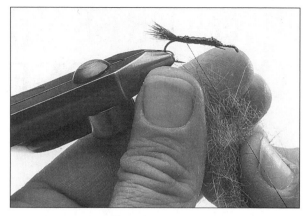

1. After tying the tail and underbody as shown on Chuck's Golden Stone form a dubbing noodle around the thread with a clump of dubbing. Page 144, steps 1-5.

2. Form a dubbing loop with the thread as shown.

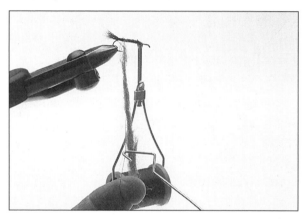

3. Hook a strand of the loop with a Cal Bird dubbing tool and remove your finger.

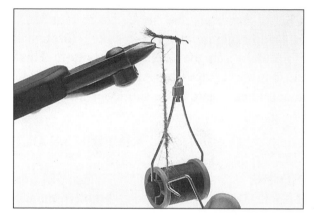

4. Spin the loop to produce a fuzzy yarn.

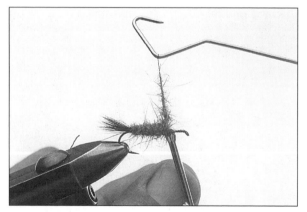

5. Using the dubbing tool wrap the body forward and secure with thread.

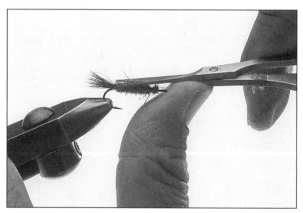

6. Trim excess dubbing on the top and bottom of the fly, not the sides.

7. Measure a stacked bundle of elk hair to extend to the tip of the tail. Note that the bundle is relatively sparse.

8. Tie the bundle in with the tips forward as shown. Trim the butts and wrap over with thread. This will form both the underwing and head.

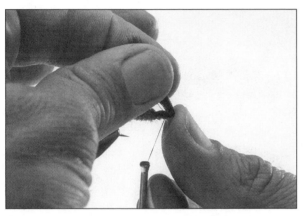

9. Cement the tie in point. Push the hair back against the thread with the thumb and positioning it on top of the hook with the fingers.

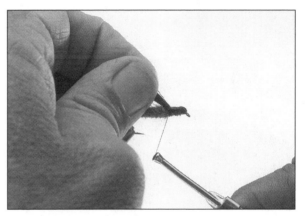

10. Wrap back over the hair to the body as shown. Flare the wing with your thumb as in Chuck"s Golden Stone. Page 146, step 13.

11. Stack a sparse bundle of calf tail for the overwing. The overwing should be the length of the body.

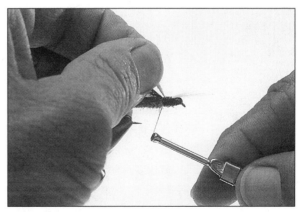

12. Tie in the overwing and trim the butts. The overwing should not flare and should only extend to the end of the body.

13. Tie in the hackle just in front of the wing. Cement the tie in area then wrap the hackle to the point shown.

14. After tying off and trimming the hackle, whip finish behind the eye and in front of the hair head. Trim the bottom of the hackle flush.

15. Side view of the finished Riverbend Stone.

16. Bottom view showing the sparseness of the wing.

CDC CADDIS

Jay Buchner

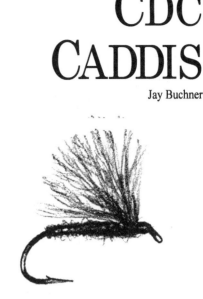

A few years ago I saw the first information and patterns using CDC (Cul de Canard) feathers. Immediately, two questions bothered me. First, why hadn't I thought to use this material, and second, how many pounds of CDC had I not collected in my years of hunting waterfowl. During the ensuing waterfowl seasons I solved my supply problem by collecting nicely plumed CDC feathers from wild ducks and geese.

In the winter months that followed hunting season, I received some commercially produced CDC feathers. They were sparsely plumed compared to their wild counterparts. I also started noticing bad reviews about CDC. The reviews would say that the material didn't float, and it rapidly fell apart when fished. This prompted my curiosity, but my CDC tests were delayed until I had more time on my hands.

While on a fishing trip to Yellowstone National Park in the spring of '91, a small Ziploc bag of CDC feathers fell out of my tying kit just when I was setting up to wrap some caddis. On impulse I dashed off three or four simple caddis (just as described in the tying instructions of this book). The trout took them with relish. The CDC Caddis floated well (I applied floatant to the body, not the wing, and blotted the water from the CDC, then false cast between fish), and it held up well after eight or ten fish.

The CDC Caddis is tied to imitate an adult, but may be taken as a captive emerger or spent caddis because it rides low in the surface film. What the trout perceive it as depends on the time of day and possibly what's happening on the stream. Any adult pattern which can cross over into the emerger or spent group provides a big advantage to the angler.

In my opinion it is essential to use CDC from wild waterfowl, which will ensure both durability and flotation. I continue to enjoy success with the CDC Caddis as well as a few other CDC patterns I now tie.

CDC CADDIS

HOOK:	Mustad 94845 or equivalent, sizes 12-22
THREAD:	6/0 or 8/0 olive
BODY:	Olive fine poly dubbing
WING:	2 CDC (Cul-de-Canard) feathers

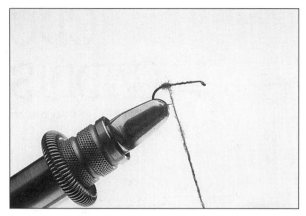

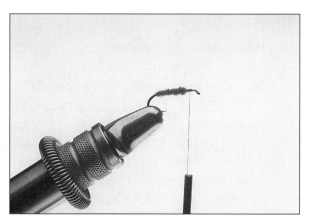

1. Begin dubbing a body above the barb of the hook.

2. Dub forward forming a body as shown.

3. Select a pair of CDC feathers for the wing.

4. Tie in with the tips extending just over the bend of the hook.

5. The finished CDC Caddis.

Cranefly Larva
Tied by Joe Burke

Furimsky's Nymph
Tied by Joe Burke

Carey Special
Tied by Jay Buchner

Black Martinez
Tied by Jack Dennis

Olive Serendipity
Tied by Mike Lawson

Rusty Serendipity
Tied by Mike Lawson

Butler Caddis
Tied by Jack Dennis

All Rounder Mayfly Nymph
Tied by John Barr

All Rounder Damsel Nymph
Tied by John Barr

All Rounder Dragonfly Nymph
Tied by John Barr

Olive Net Builder
Tied by John Barr

Cream Net Builder
Tied by John Barr

Barr Golden Stone
Tied by John Barr

Barr Dark Stone
Tied by John Barr

Golden Burlap Nymph
Tied by Chuck Stranahan

George's Rubber Leg Brown Stone
Tied by Joe Burke

Chuck's Light Caddis Variant
Tied by Scott Sanchez

Dun Caddis Variant
Tied by Joe Burke

Green Caddis Variant
Tied by Joe Burke

Blind Angler'sd Caddis Variant
Tied by Scott Sanchez

EMERGERS, CRIPPLES & STILLBORNS

Parachute Midge Emerger
Tied by Gary Wilmott

Minimal Mayfly
Tied by Ralph Headrick

Green Drake Quigley Cripple
Tied by Joe Burke

Brown Drake Quigley Cripple
Tied by Joe Burke

Mahogany Quigley Cripple
Tied by Joe Burke

PT Quigley Cripple
Tied by Joe Burke

Biot Quigley Cripple
Tied by Joe Burke

Barr Emerger PMD
Tied by John Barr

Blue Wing Olive Barr Emerger
Tied by Joe Burke

All Rounder Caddis Pupa
Tied by John Barr

Twitch Pause Nymph
Tied by Chuck Stranahan

X-Caddis
Tied by Jay Buchner

Pale Morning Dun PT Emerger
Tied by Mike Lawson

Jay's Humpback Emerger
Tied by Jay Buchner

Halo Emerger
Tied by Gary LaFontaine

Mess
Tied by Gary LaFontaine

AQUATIC ADULT INSECTS

Cut-Wing Callabaetis
Tied by Pat Berry

Cut-Wing Flavilinea
Tied by Pat Berry

Parachute Hare's Ear
Tied by Scott Sanchez

Loop Wing Adams
Tied by Scott Sanchez

Thorax Dun
Tied by Mike Lawson

No-Hackle
Tied by Mike Lawson

Pale Morning Dun Comparadun
Tied by Jay Buchner

Chuck's Salmonfly
Tied by Chuck Stranahan

Chuck's Golden Stone
Tied by Chuck Stranahan

Riverbend Olive Stone
Tied by Chuck Stranahan

CDC Caddis
Tied by Jay Buchner

Hemingway Caddis
Tied by Mike Lawson

Chuck's Light Caddis Variant
Tied by Chuck Stranahan

Dun Caddis Variant
Tied by Chuck Stranahan

Green Caddis Variant
Tied by Chuck Stranahan

Blind Angler's Caddis Variant
Tied by Chuck Stranahan

Charcoal Hair Body Caddis
Tied by Larry Walker

Speckled Hair Body Caddis
Tied by Larry Walker

Adult Cranefly
Tied by Jay Buchner

EGG LAYING ADULTS

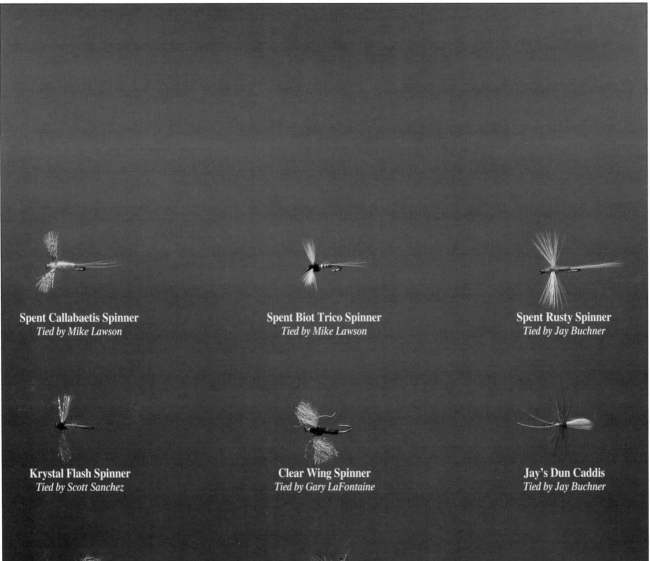

Spent Callabaetis Spinner
Tied by Mike Lawson

Spent Biot Trico Spinner
Tied by Mike Lawson

Spent Rusty Spinner
Tied by Jay Buchner

Krystal Flash Spinner
Tied by Scott Sanchez

Clear Wing Spinner
Tied by Gary LaFontaine

Jay's Dun Caddis
Tied by Jay Buchner

Diving Caddis
Tied by Gary LaFontaine

Spent Partridge Caddis
Tied by Mike Lawson

Spent Midge
Tied by Mike Lawson

ATTRACTORS

Pepperoni Yuk Bug
Tied by Bruce James

Turck Tarantula (standard)
Tied by Guy Turck

Turck Tarantula (brown)
Tied by Guy Turck

J.J. Special
Tied by Jimmy Jones

Black Legged Waterwalker
Tied by Bruce E. James

Airhead
Tied by Justin Baker

Mohawk
Tied by Heather LaFontaine

Wild Thing Mohawk
Tied by Heather LaFontaine

Creature
Tied by Gary LaFontaine

Double Wing
Tied by Gary LaFontaine

Chuck's Peacock Trude
Tied by Chuck Stranahan

Chuck's Hare's Ear Trude
Tied by Chuck Stranahan

Chuck's Yellow Trude
Tied by Chuck Stranahan

Seducer (orange
Tied by Randall Kaufmann

Seducer (black)
Tied by Randall Kaufmann

Seducer (yellow & orange)
Tied by Randall Kaufmann

Seducer (with hair overwing)
Tied by Randall Kaufmann

Seducer (little yellow)
Tied by Randall Kaufmann

Improved Royal Humpy
Tied by Jack Dennis

Double Humpy
Tied by Joe Burke

Mutant Ninja Cicada
Tied by Emmett Heath

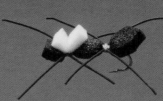

Chernobyl Ant
Tied by Emmett Heath

Bear Brown No-Hackle Ant
Tied by Bear McKinney

Harvest Beetle
Tied by Dan Storm

Hair Beetle
Tied by Jack Dennis

Jay-Dave's Hopper
Tied by Jay Buchner

Flat Creek Hopper
Tied by Ralph Headrick

Larry's Swimming Leech
Tied by Larry Walker

Cross-Cut Scud
Tied by Joe Burke

Snake River Muddler
Tied by Jay Buchner

Double Bunny
Tied by Scott Sanchez

HEMINGWAY CADDIS

Mike Lawson

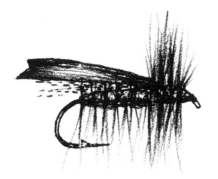

Many people are aware that the Hemingway Caddis is named after Jack Hemingway, but few know the rest of the story behind this deadly adult caddis pattern.

Back in the early 70's, Jack would take a May trip over to the Henry's Fork to fish about the time of the Mother's Day caddis hatch. Before coming he would get in touch with René Harrop and order a medium dun or gray colored caddis pattern similar to a Henryville Special. René would tie up a bunch of the flies for Jack, who would be satisfied and go off fishing.

At this same time I was teaching school and my wife; Sheralee and I were doing a lot of commercial tying on the side. Doug Swisher had put us in touch with a fellow named Cal Gates on Michigan's famous Ausable River. We would tie about 3,000 dozen flies a year for Cal. He would call us up and describe the different caddis on the Ausable and we would tie variations of the Henryville Special in different colors to fill his orders.

In 1977 when René and I were opening the Henry's Fork Angler Fly Shop in Last Chance, Idaho, we sat down and figured out which dry caddis patterns we should feature. We filled the spent egg laying adult niche with a pattern Sheralee invented called the Spent Partridge Caddis. To cover the adult niche we decided on a pattern similar to the ones René tied for Jack, which wasn't much different than what we had done for Cal.

Jack's early season flies were much lighter in shade than our fly, which over the years has become even darker. For lack of a name for the fly, we called it a Hemingway Caddis. I never got around to asking Jack if it was all right to use his name, but one day he came into the shop and bought a whole bunch of them, so we took that as a sign of his approval.

I've received great reports on the success of the Hemingway Caddis from the Bighorn and Yellowstone Rivers. It should work anywhere you see dark caddis. If you stock only two dry caddis patterns in your fly box, make sure the Hemingway Caddis is one of them, and the Spent Partridge Caddis is the other one.

HEMINGWAY CADDIS

HOOK:	Tiemco 100, Dai-Riki 305 or equivalent, sizes 12-20
THREAD:	6/0 olive
BODY HACKLE:	Med to dark dun neck feather
BODY:	Olive fine poly dubbing
UNDERWING:	Wood duck flank feather
OVERWING:	Mallard duck wing feather
THORAX:	Peacock herl 3-4 strands
HACKLE:	Same as body hackle

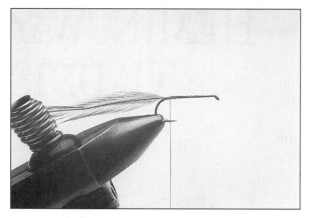

1. Attach a dun hackle feather with dull side toward you to the top of the hook.

2. Dub a slightly tapered abdomen 2/3 up the hook shank.

3. Palmer the hackle forward through the abdomen and trim the stem.

4. Measure the wood duck flank feather for the underwing. Length is 1/3 beyond the bend of the hook.

5. Tie the tips of the flank feather in as shown and trim the butt of the feather.

6. Select the mallard quill feather fibers for the overwing. Length should be well beyond the underwing which will be trimmed later.

7. Double over the feather fibers and tie in as shown.

8. Trim the wing feather at an angle to form a ' V '. The overwing will be the same length as the underwing.

9. Tie in 1 or 2 hackle feathers depending on the size of the fly.

10. Attach 3 or 4 strands of peacock herl by the tips and wrap a thorax.

11. Palmer the hackle through the thorax. Tie off, trim and whip finish.

12. The finished Hemingway Caddis.

CHUCK'S CADDIS VARIANT

Chuck Stranahan

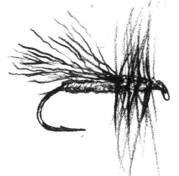

The Caddis Variants, known among their fans as everything from Caddis Various to Stranahan's Deviants, but more often simply as CV's, are the deadliest and most consistently productive dry flies I have ever fished. In fact, I estimate that fully half of the trout I have taken on dry flies have come on the Light Caddis Variant, the fly shown in the tying sequence here.

Despite their delicate appearance they are extremely durable. A thirty fish session with one fly is not uncommon. They are easy to tie, once the hair flaring technique employed in winging the fly is mastered. As a body-wing-hackle "three step" dry fly, it's easy to turn out a fair supply of CV's in short order.

Why are Caddis Variants so effective? I think it has to do with putting a believable shape/silhouette over the trout. The proportions of the fly mimic the proportions of nature, not those defined by fly tying tradition. CV's can be fished dead drift, twitched, danced, or pulled under and fished as the underwater egg-laying stage of some caddis. They fish equally well in both flat and rough water.

The fly came into being one spring day during the mid-sixties. I had gone to the banks of the Sacramento River in Redding, California for that refurbishment of spirit which comes to me only from moving water and natural surroundings. I watched steelhead tearing into the nests of salmon, raiding eggs and the fry that were just coming out of the sand, while the big, tired old male salmon chased them off.

As the morning sun climbed higher in the sky and the water temperature rose, a caddis hatch started to come off. There were a lot of flies. They would settle on the surface, then fly slowly upstream with their wings brushing the water for a distance of eight or nine inches, then settle to the water's surface again. The steelhead began to drop to the tail of the run to take the adult insects with violent riseforms.

I watched for a long time, thinking of an old A.J. McClane article, "Walking the Dry Fly" from *Field and Stream*. In it, he suggests moving the fly slowly upstream a few inches at a time, using the rod tip for control, and letting the fly settle and drift between movements. I knew this method would work here. The movement would mimic the behavior of the caddis. All that was needed was a suitable fly.

I caught a natural and looked at it from underneath as a fish would. The venation of the wings scattered light. The wing length was about twice the body length, which in turn was well defined and chubby. The wings didn't end at the abdomen, as they do in many traditional dry flies.

I rushed home to incorporate these characteristics into an imitation that might fool those aggressive steelhead. I tied an Adams-like fly using dyed blue dun hackle I had obtained from Cal Bird. With a dozen of these prototype CV's and my Shakespeare Wonderrod, I headed back to the stream.

That dozen CV's was soon lost to the takes of powerful steelhead. Adapting to a slip-strike technique, I held some of the fish for a while, even landed a few. Some, when hooked, fired their afterburners and headed for the Golden Gate, some 250 river miles distant. My old Pflueger Medalist didn't hold that much backing.

As I have refined the fly over the years, I have noted repeatedly that too short a hackle or too full a hackle collar will diminish the fly's effectiveness. A wing that isn't flared will not blend into the hackle collar and will look unnatural from beneath.

A chubby body of the right color and size, suspended in a halo of hackle collar and flared wing, simulate the color and motion of the beating wings of a caddis. My Caddis Variant series has a sparse flared wing over a well defined body to mimic these proportions and create the silhouette of a natural.

Over the years, I have enjoyed tying a Light Caddis Variant on the line of more than one client. Their initial skepticism of using a new pattern is replaced with enthusiasm by day's end. I know, at that point, that the angler is well on his way to becoming a member of the growing and dedicated underground army of devotees which the CV has garnered. It's that kind of a bug.

NOTE: Chuck's Caddis Variant is commercially available from Umpqua Feather Merchants.

CHUCK'S LIGHT CADDIS VARIANT

HOOK:	Tiemco 921, Dai-Riki 305 or equivalent, sizes 8-20
THREAD:	6/0 or 8/0 yellow
BODY:	Yellow poly dubbing
WING:	Short, fine deer hair, natural color to blend with hackle
HACKLE:	Spencer light ginger dyed grizzly hackle

NOTE: Colors of thread, dubbed body, hackle, the shade of hair wing or hook size can be varied to create Dun, Cinnamon, Ginger, Dark or Giant Orange Caddis Variants. Adapt to match your caddis hatches.

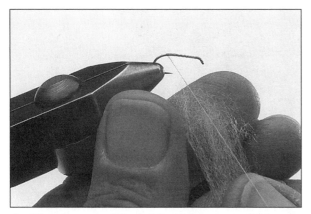

1. Wrap unwaxed thread from the eye to the bend of the hook and cement. By pinching with your fingers flatten dubbing under the thread.

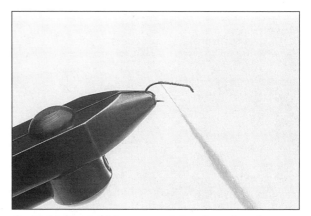

2. Fold the dubbing around the thread to form a noodle.

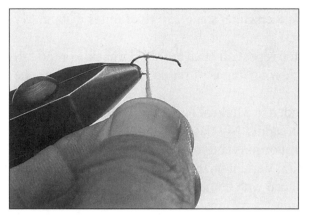

3. Slide the dubbing noodle up the thread to the hook shank. Twist and roll with fingers to tighten it into a rope.

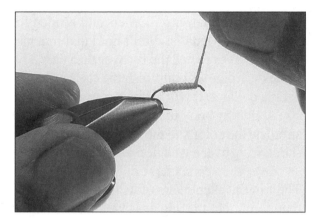

4. Wrap the rope of dubbing into a segmented body.

5. Select, clean and stack a small bunch of fine textured deer hair for the wing. The wing is twice the body length.

6. Tie the hair in tightly at the front of the body then secure with loose wraps to the middle of the hook shank. Hair should not flare from the thread tension. Trim butts.

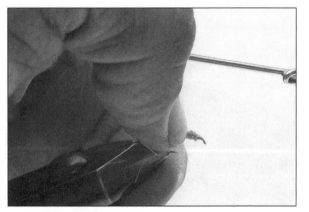

7. Gently push down with your thumb to flare the hair laterally at mid-hook and secure with a few tight wraps of thread.

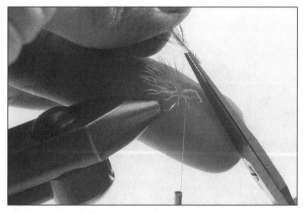

8. Wrap over the trimmed butts to form a base for the hackle. Prepare hackle feather as shown.

9. Cement area and hackle. Trim the tag end and whip finish.

10. Finished Chuck's Caddis Variant.

HAIR BODY CADDIS

Larry Walker

We watch in awe as the "masters" spin, stack, insert, stripe, patch and flare deer hair. The use of this productive and inexpensive material has always been impressive to fly tiers. Selecting the right hair for the right job is extremely important. The video tape, *Tying Western Trout Flies*, by Jack Dennis, which explains hair for specific uses, is a must.

I created the Dubbit tool to solve problems of loop dubbing furs and blends when tying scuds, leech patterns and the thorax segments of stoneflies and Gold Ribbed Hare's Ears. The use of the Dubbit to loop spin deer hair is now one of it's major functions. Deer hair is no longer the mystery material of the "masters".

Hair bodied caddis patterns have been inside my little old bald head for sometime. I'm glad to finally have this opportunity to share them with you.

I believe I have found a sensible place to use the Cul de Canard (CDC) feather. Many of the applications I have seen make absolutely no sense. I've tied the Hair Body Caddis without the CDC and the profiling just isn't right. My success has been so great using the CDC for the underwing on my Hair Body Caddis, that I am experimenting with it on hoppers, cicada and beetles. The early results are impressive.

Options for the Hair Body Caddis include an egg butt, antennae and a visual aid I call a "wheresidat".

The egg butt section is created by dubbing dyed deer hair into the rear of the fly. My favorite color is yellow, but red or light green will also work.

Monofilament works well for the antennae because it is readily available and durable. It easily accepts dyes or ink from marking pens so you can create a wide range of shades. One alternative to monofilament for the antennae is Gary LaFontaine's moustache hair. Collecting that material might pose a problem, so take along two big guys and a rope.

I hope you find that tying the Hair Body Caddis is both interesting and educational. The process of learning how to spin hair with the Dubbit tool takes a little practice, but it is much easier than you might think. The technique can be used to spin hair on the bodies of very small Irresistibles as well as other flies. The finished fly will be durable and catch fish.

HAIR BODY CADDIS

HOOK:	Tiemco 5212 or equivalent, sizes 10-18
THREAD:	6/0 or 8/0 iron gray
BODY:	Natural deer body hair
UNDERWING:	Dun CDC feather, mottled preferred
OVERWING:	Section from mallard duck feather
HACKLE:	Depending on hook size, one or two med to dark dun or dun dyed grizzly neck hackles, one size larger than hook size

1. Align the cleaned deer hair as shown so it can be easily picked up when needed.

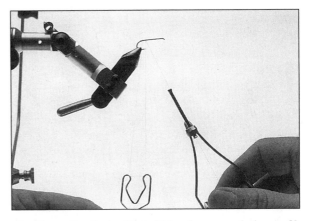

2. Form the first of 2 dubbing loops and close off the thread gap at the hook shank. Wrap the thread forward approximately 1/4 inch and create a second dubbing loop.

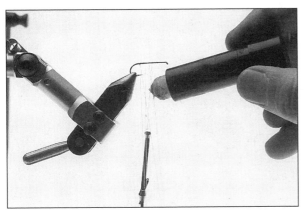

3. Apply dubbing wax and spread evenly with your fingers to all four strands. Wipe off excess.

4. Insert deer butts first into the double loop. Don't push it all the way up to the hook shank, leave room.

5. Pinch with finger and thumb to position. Do not allow any of the hair to lay across other hairs, they should be parallel to each other.

6. Close the thread gaps in the loop by passing the bobbin around the 4 strands. Rotate the bobbin 10 to 12 times to close the double loop behind the hair.

7. The above step may be helpful when getting started: use wire tester style hackle pliers to keep the loops from unwinding.

8. You can trim the hair even at both sides at this point.

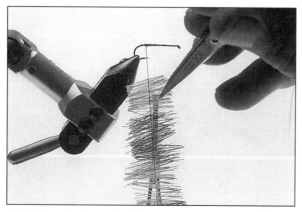

9. Point of scissors indicates where hair is crossing over, this must be straig2htened out before you can spin the hair.

10. Spin the dubbing tool numerous turns to create a bottle brush appearance as shown.

11. Wrap the spun hair to form a body as shown, pulling back the hair of the previous wrap with fingers before each new wrap.

12. After spinning 2/3 of the way up the hook shank, whip finish and cut the thread. Pick out flat spots with the bodkin.

13. Trim to shape with scissors. This is a good point to stage tie a number of these flies too.

14. Reattach thread then tie in CDC underwing as shown.

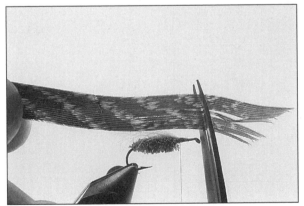

15. Cut out a section from either a mallard wing feather or turkey tail. Even the tips that will be tied in.

16. Tie in the overwing in front of the body by the tips and cut an angle to produce a ' V ' wing 1/2 hook shank beyond the bend of the hook.

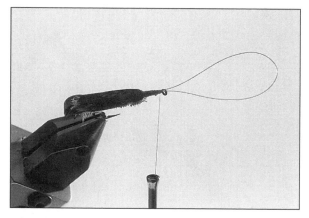

17. Tie in a loop of mono as shown if antennae are desired.

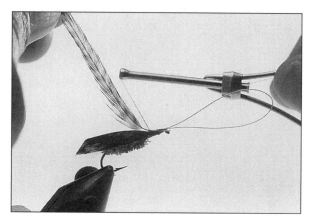

18. Tie in 1 or 2 neck feathers one size larger than the hook size.

19. Wrap the hackle and whip finish.

20. Cut the mono loop with the scissors to form the antennae.

21. The finished Hair Body Caddis.

ADULT CRANEFLY

Jack Dennis

This big Diptera looks like a giant mosquito. Its importance is overlooked by many western fishermen. Because mornings are generally quite cool in the mountains, most hatch activity and trout feeding starts about mid-morning. Consequently, few if any anglers venture out at the crack of dawn to fish here. But, for those who venture out on the stream before the full sun hits the water, an adult cranefly skating across the edge of an undercut bank or pool can elicit a dramatic response. I'm not talking about a sipping take; fish really leap for this fly and the angler's first response is usually to strike quickly. Be slow in your strike or you will miss most if not all of these crashing takes.

Although this fly is most effective in the early morning, it can be used as a searching pattern during the day when no other activity is apparent. Be sure to cover the area fished with repeated casts. When you see the natural adult in action, it seems to trace the same route back and forth over the water. Drift or cast the fly down a run, edge or pool and skip or skate it back toward you.

Tie this pattern sparse, because the natural is very slight. The wings, gangly legs, and body length are its key features, so keep these characteristics in mind when you have that fine wire hook in your vise. Jay Buchner has a cranefly pattern that is time-proven to be deadly. After tying some of these, you might just be tempted to get up a little earlier to catch the activity.

ADULT CRANEFLY

HOOK:	Mustad 94840, Dai-Riki 305 or equivalent, sizes 8-14
THREAD:	3/0 tan monocord
BODY:	4 strand poly yarn; remove a strand for sizes 10 and smaller
WINGS:	Dun hackle feathers
HACKLE:	Dun saddle hackle, oversized X2

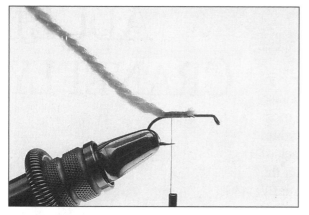

1. Tie in the four strand poly yarn to the rear 1/2 of the hook shank.

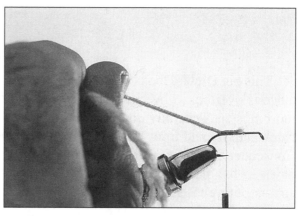

2. Twist with the thumb and forefinger to form a rope.

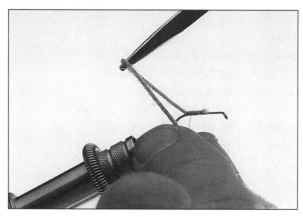

3. Using forceps, loop this rope as shown.

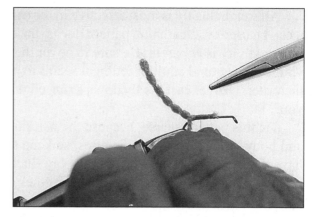

4. When you remove the forceps the yarn will twist on itself. The free end of the yarn can now be secured to the hook shank. Do not cut the tag end of the yarn.

5. Tie in the hackle tips for the wings at point shown.

6. Tie in the saddle hackle right behind the wings and divide the wings with the thread.

7. Wrap the yarn forward to the eye. Tie off and trim.

8. Palmer the hackle behind and in front of the wings. Whip finish.

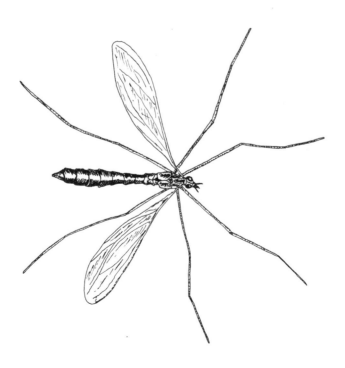

9. Finished Adult Cranefly.

EGG LAYING
ADULTS

SPINNERS

Mike Lawson

Few fly fishermen relate the significance of spent mayfly spinners to selectively feeding trout. That is probably because the spent spinners float flush in the surface film and they aren't easily seen by the angler.

Spent mayfly spinners are easier to see on lakes and can literally cover the water. Trout which cruise along feeding on the spents are called gulpers. It can be a lot of fun float tubing when the gulpers are up on Hebgen Lake just out of West Yellowstone, Montana.

These flies can also cover the water in spring creeks, where trout will sit with their heads into the current and often roll back and forth popping their heads up to sip the passing spents. If you pay attention to the feeding rhythm of the fish, you can have plenty of action in this situation.

The same thing happens on big freestone rivers like the Madison and Yellowstone. Here, most fishermen don't have a clue as to what the fish are taking, because the fish are usually in the broken water of riffles where you can't see the spents. If you see these fish stacked in the riffles, it is easy to think they are taking emerging insects. Well, sometimes they are on spent mayflies.

A spent mayfly pattern can be impossible to see in a riffle. A parachute wing can help you see it, as well as help float the fly. The wing has to be shorter than standard parachute wings (1/2 the body length) so it isn't the first thing the trout will see on the fly. If it is too tall it will make the fly look like a dun and it won't trigger the right response from the fish. I can remember when Orvis used a little fluorescent indicator tied on top of their spent spinner patterns. It really was easier to see them in the water.

The hue of the wing is very important. White is a good contrast to a body color for the fisherman and tier, but not always for the fish. In my experience a medium gray is a real good neutral color. Remember, you are looking down at the spinner on the water and seeing it against the dark background of the bottom. It's the opposite for the trout. They are looking up at the fly against the bright background of the surface and sky. They see a neutral hue better. Any material or floatant that can create air bubbles can make the fly appear even more natural.

There are a variety of ways to tie spent mayfly spinners. All should have slender bodies. Some of the ties, such as *Tricos* and *Callibaetis* are species specific, while other ties are more generic. I am going to show you how to tie a Spent Callibaetis Spinner and a Spent Biot Trico Spinner which work well on the Henry's Fork and the waters in our area.

SPENT CALLIBAETIS SPINNER

HOOK: Tiemco 100, Dai-Riki 305 or equivalent, sizes 14-18

THREAD: 6/0 or 8/0 tan

TAIL: Dun hackle fibers

WING: One right, one left gray partridge body feather

BODY: Cream colored fine poly dubbing

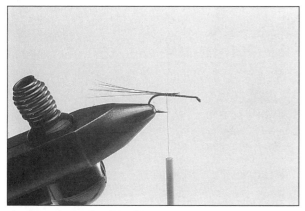

1. Attach the hackle fibers for the tail 1 1/2 hook shanks long.

2. Divide the tails with a couple of wraps of thread under and behind the fibers which lifts and flares.

3. At mid-shank, tie in a pair of partridge back feathers with tips forward. Place the feathers back to back. The wing should be a hook shank in length.

4. Stand the wings up with thread wraps as shown.

5. Divide the wings by figure eighting with the thread.

6. Dub a tapered body from the tail to the head wrapping the dubbing to the base of the wing and not figure eighting through the wing. Whip Finish.

7. The finished Spent Callibaetis Spinner. Note the taper as tapered bodies are important with spent mayfly spinners.

SPENT BIOT TRICO SPINNER

HOOK:	Tiemco 100, Dai-Riki 305 or equivalent, sizes 18-28
THREAD:	8/0 black
TAIL:	Dun hackle fibers
BODY:	Natural goose biot
THORAX:	Black fine poly dubbing
WINGS:	One right, one left hen hackle feather tips

1. Attach the tail fibers the same way as on the Callibaetis Spinner. Page 171, step 1.

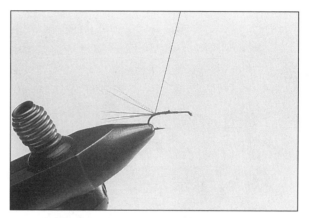

2. Divide the tail as on the Callibaetis Spinner. Page 171, step 2.

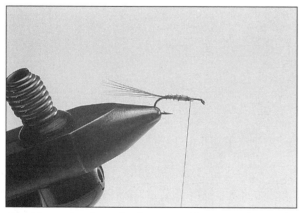

3. After tying in a single goose biot wrap forward with hackle pliers and tie off to get the segmented and tapered look shown.

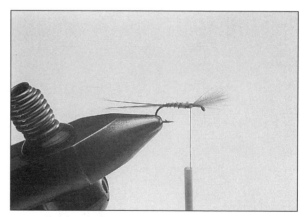

4. Tie the tips of a pair of hen hackle feathers forward. They should be one hook shank in length.

5. Stand the wings up with thread.

6. Separate and flatten the wings by figure eighting with thread.

7. Dub a thorax from behind the wing to in front of the wing. Make tight wraps at the base of the wings but do not figure eight through the wings. Whip finish.

8. Finished Spent Biot Trico Spinner.

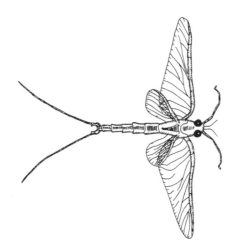

KRYSTAL FLASH SPINNER

Scott Sanchez

The spent spinner stage of the mayfly is an important food item to trout. Because spent spinners cannot escape, the trout can get very selective towards them.

From a fisherman's standpoint, spent spinner patterns are effective, but hard to see. Most anglers feel more confident with a fly they can see, and confidence is an important part of fishing. If you can see the fly, you can usually get a better drift with it.

George Harvey started tying Trico spinners using Krystal Flash for the tough Pennsylvania spring creeks he fishes. My experiences with his patterns have all been good. The Krystal Flash wings, from a fisherman's perspective, really stand out in contrast to the stream bottom. Looking up from the trout's viewpoint, the wing looks clear against the bright background of the undersurface of the water and the sky. This is the same appearance the natural spinner has.

I have had especially good luck using Krystal Flash Spinners during Trico activity on the Snake River in Jackson Hole. Krystal Flash wings applied to Rusty Spinners have produced good results everywhere I have fished them, including on those telepathic trout on the Henry's Fork. This is a good pattern to add to your fly arsenal.

KRYSTAL FLASH SPINNER

HOOK:	Dai-Riki 305, 310 or equivalent, sizes 16-22
THREAD:	8/0 light gray
TAIL:	Clear or gray Microfibetts
ABDOMEN:	Light olive sparkle dubbing such as Scintilla
RIBBING:	Light gray 8/0 thread from dubbing loop
THORAX:	Scintilla #46 peacockle dubbing or similar peacock sparkle blend
UNDERWING:	Clear Antron or CDC for variety
OVERWING:	Pearl Krystal Flash

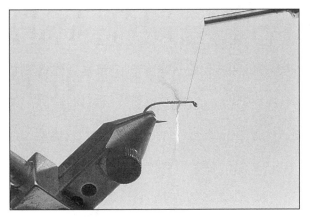

1. Tie in Antron underwing across the hook in position shown. CDC may be substituted.

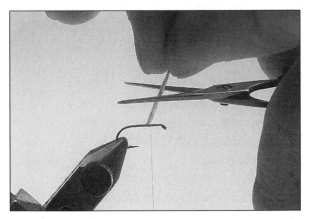

2. The Krystal Flash overwing is tied in directly over the underwing. Pull both wings upright and trim to length.

3. Throw a dubbing loop with the thread at the tail of the fly.

4. Tie in 4 to 6 Microfibetts as a long tail and split by pressing down on the base of the tail with the fingernail of the index finger. * See footnote, page177.

5. Pull the dubbing loop through the divided tail and tie down with thread wraps do not cut the loop at this point.

6. After dubbing a tapered body to the rear of the wing, rib with the dubbing loop.

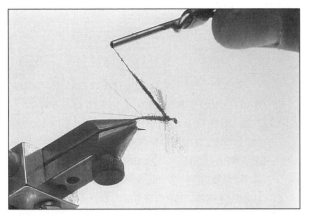

7. Apply more dubbing to the thread and figure eight through the wings. Whip finish.

8. The finished Krystal Flash Spinner.

* The wing and material used in this fly are very translucent and hence very difficult to photograph. The tail splitting technique may be more clear to you on the tying sequences for the Parachute Hare's Ear, pages 126-127, steps 5-7.

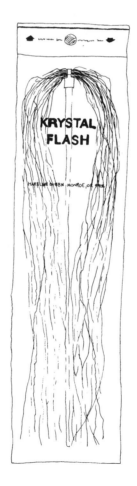

SPENT MAYFLY-RUSTY SPINNER

Jay Buchner

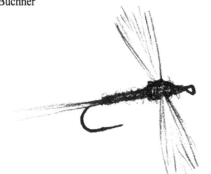

I learned fly tying from my grandfather when I was eight years old. Soon I was copying the drawings and photos of patterns I found in books, as well as using my imagination. Some years later, I read Ernest Schwiebert's *Matching the Hatch*. It had great pattern lists, but I was disappointed to find there were no photos of the author's finished flies. My imagination was of no help here.

Years passed and I began professionally tying custom patterns for a local shop. Finally the mystery of Schwiebert's patterns was solved. The shop owner had several special patterns he said were from *Matching the Hatch* and were in fact tied by the author. He went on about how effective they were, which only compounded my serious interest of finally seeing what had been so well written about.

Of the group of flies, all were interesting and several unique. One particular fly, a wrapped hackle spinner, caught my eye. When I tied this pattern for the shop owner's order, several extras or rejects made their way into my fly box. The effectiveness of this surface film imitation immediately impressed me, as did it's durability and floatability. The Spent Mayfly is my favorite pattern when mayfly spinners are on the water.

SPENT MAYFLY RUSTY SPINNER

HOOK:	Mustad 94845 or equivalent, sizes 14-18
THREAD:	6/0 or 8/0 rust color
TAIL:	Microfibetts tied long
BODY:	Rust colored fine poly dubbing
HACKLE:	White or light dun neck hackle, oversized at least 2 hook gapes

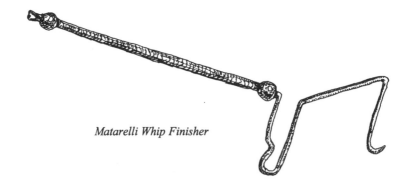

Matarelli Whip Finisher

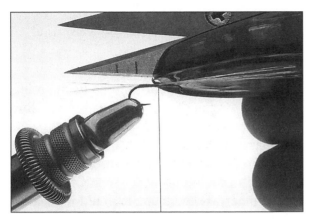

1. Tie a Microfibett tail long (at least 1 1/2 shank lengths).

2. Tie in a neck feather for the hackle, it should be oversized at least 2 hook gapes.

3. Make about 3 to 4 wraps of hackle from mid shank forward.

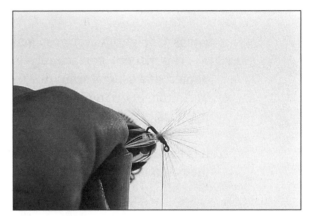

4. Divide hackle with the fingers and figure eight with the thread to create right and left spent wings.

5. Dub a tapered body from the tail to the head. Figure eight the dubbing through the hackle. Whip finish.

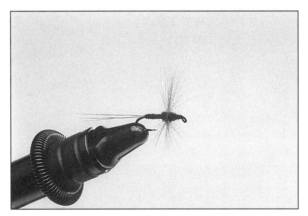

6. Finished Spent Rusty Spinner.

CLEAR WING SPINNER

Gary LaFontaine

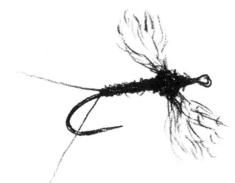

This fly was born on the giant spring creek stretch of the Missouri River below Holter Dam. That Montana water, with massive spinner falls of Trico mayflies from July through September, served as a tough proving ground. If the Clear Wing Spinner worked there, it would work anywhere.

The Clear Wing Spinner subsequently became a standard on rivers all over the country, but not just because it is a wonderful imitation. Anglers embrace it for the practical reason that they can see it. The wings of bright clear Antron make the fly, even a size 18 or 20, visible thirty feet away.

This pattern has actually grown beyond its primary role, having also become popular as a general searching fly. Those sparkling wings, with all the natural attraction of Antron, help it pull trout to the surface any time, not just when they are sipping spent mayflies.

Without a doubt this is my favorite spent mayfly pattern. Once anglers see how easy it is to tie and how effective it is when fished, it will become an all-around favorite of theirs too.

CLEAR WING SPINNER

HOOK:	Dai-Riki 300 or equivalent, sizes 10-22
THREAD:	8/0, color not critical
TAIL:	Dark dun hackle fibers
WING:	Clear Antron
BODY:	Synthetic dubbing such as Scintilla to match natural; cream, olive, gray, black and brownish red are com mon colors

Griffin Ceramic Bobbin

1. Split the hackle fiber tail using the same thread loop technique used in the Krystal Flash Spinner. Page 176, steps 3 and 5. Cut the dubbing loop after splitting the tail.

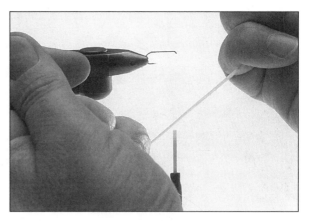

2. Stretch the clear Antron material as shown to take some of the kink out of it.

3. Tie in the Antron across the hook securing with figure eight thread wraps.

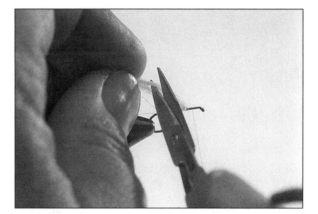

4. Grab both ends of the wings and cut to length all at once.

5. Sparsely dub the thread as shown.

6. Wrap the dubbing forward to the base of the wing.

7. Figure eight through the wings with the dubbing to build a thorax. Whip finish.

8. Finished Clear Wing Spinner.

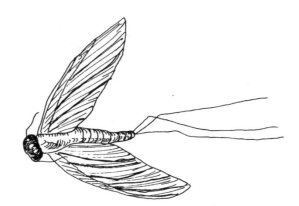

JAY'S DUN CADDIS

This pattern was originally introduced in 1978 in *The Second Fly Tyer's Almanac*. A number of tyers, including yours truly, were challenged to produce several unique fly patterns utilizing seldom used feathers from a rooster skin. Jay's Dun Caddis stands out as the most consistent pattern from this challenge.

Although it has not caught on as a popular fly with the angling public, I continue to get rave reviews every year from those who have recognized its niche in their fly boxes.

The Dun Caddis, as described, is an excellent imitation for a dry caddis and works well during hatches. However, it really earns it's keep as a spent caddis. This all to often overlooked part of the caddis cycle is coped with quite well using Jay's Dun Caddis. Spent caddis, or for that matter any spent spinners or crippled insects will stack up in quiet eddies. If your stalk is true and you're observant, you will notice that sipping trout are also stacked up in these eddies. In your excitement, try not to line them with the first cast.

JAY'S DUN CADDIS

HOOK:	Mustad 94845 or equivalent, sizes 8-20
THREAD:	6/0 or 8/0 gray
BODY:	Goose secondary wing feather fibers
WING:	Dun body feathers from a rooster or hen
ANTENNAE:	Stems of wing feathers
HACKLE:	Dun neck hackle, oversized x2

1. Select a matching pair of dun body feathers from a rooster or hen. These will be the wings.

2. Strip away all but the tip fibers as shown.

3. Coat with Dave's Flexament and let dry.

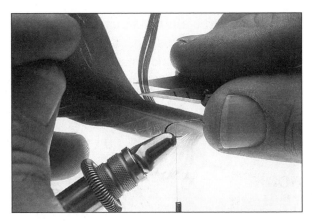

4. Cut fibers for the body from a goose secondary wing feather.

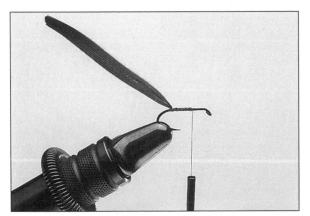

5. Tie in the goose fibers by their tips as shown.

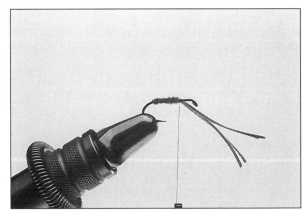

6. Wrap a slender body with the fibers as shown.

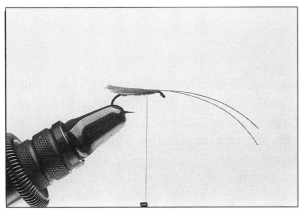

7. Tie in the wings, overlapping the body. The stems should be forward and form the antennae.

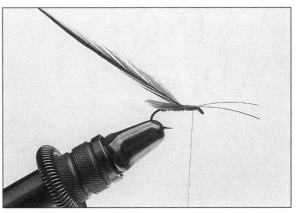

8. Cut the antennae to length. Tie on a neck hackle dull side up at the position shown.

9. Wrap the hackle forward and whip finish. Trim the top and bottom hackle fibers flat.

10. The finished Jay's Dun Caddis.

DIVING CADDIS

Gary LaFontaine

The Diving Caddis is a fly that has bucked a historical trend. Most classic downwing wet flies have faded into oblivion and are no longer commercially viable. The one exception to this is the Diving Caddis, which has become a tremendous seller.

In the summer of 1992 a large clothing store chain pushed a colorful sweatshirt that featured "fishing flies." These were beautiful pieces of clothing, sold not to anglers but to the general public (and apparently they sold well). One of the flies pictured on the shirt, along with popular modern patterns, was the Diving Caddis. This run of sweatshirts, distributed by the millions, served as the ultimate advertising vehicle, making the already good sales of the Diving Caddis boom much higher.

What does the Diving Caddis represent? Well, in many caddis species the female will dive or swim underwater to lay a string of eggs on the bottom. She carries a bright air bubble with her to survive the trip. Sometimes she makes it back to the surface and flies away; sometimes she drowns. The important thing is that she lays her eggs to perpetuate her species. The Diving Caddis imitates the adult egg-laying female underneath the water.

There is no weight on the hook shank of this fly so, although it is a wet fly, it does not go far beneath the surface. The angler fishes it with the classic wet fly method. He casts the fly across or slightly upstream, all the while keeping a slight tension on the line during the drift.

The Diving Caddis is a worthy addition to the angler's fly box. It has a specific, imitative purpose. This breaks the trend of wet flies slipping into oblivion because it catches trout in a tough feeding situation.

DIVING CADDIS

HOOK:	Dai-Riki 070 or equivalent, sizes 8-24
THREAD:	8/0 to match body color
BODY:	Ginger, bright green, russet, or grey Antron dubbing
RIBBING:	Tag end of 8/0 thread
UNDERWING:	Mallard flank, grouse or partridge feather
OVERWING:	Clear Antron
HACKLE:	Rooster neck hackle, color to match body

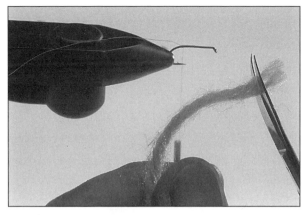

1. Attach the thread to the rear of the hook leaving the tag end to be used later for ribbing. Cut short pieces of Antron yarn as shown to make the dubbing.

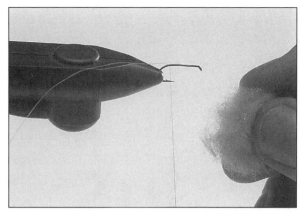

2. Touch dubbing technique shown: touch the chopped Antron dubbing to a very tacky waxed thread.

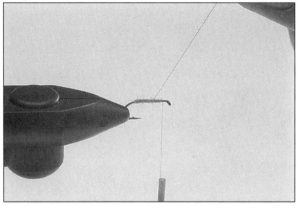

3. Wrap a very sparse body forward. Once you start to wrap forward don't overwrap previous wraps. Rib with the tag end of thread.

4. Roll the tip of a partridge feather in the fingers of the right hand as shown. This will be used as an underwing.

5. Tie in wing to extend just beyond the bend of the hook.

6. Tie in Antron overwing to extend just beyond the end of the underwing. Trim and cover with thread wraps.

7. Tie in a rooster neck feather for a hackle.

8. Wrap the hackle only 1 1/2 to 2 turns, very sparse like the body.

9. Pull back the hackle fibers with the fingers of the left hand and overwrap with thread to angle the fibers back. Whip finish.

10. Finished Diving Caddis.

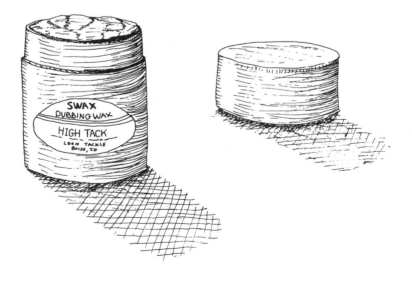

SPENT PARTRIDGE CADDIS

Mike Lawson

When Rene Harrop and I opened the Henry's Fork Angler Shop in 1977, we sat down and determined which fly patterns we needed to feature to match the insect hatches on area waters. We recognized a need for a spent caddis pattern, and I was assigned the task of developing it. Being the caring husband that I am, I immediately turned this labor of love over to my wife, Sheralee.

Sheralee tied several flies using different materials. The one we selected used a partridge feather for the wing. It not only looked best, but it outperformed any of the other flies when I field tested them. I have never found a natural material that holds it's shape better than the feathers from wild birds such as partridge and grouse. The soft speckled hackle looks buggy too. Some chicken feathers look good but don't work. When you get a partridge or grouse feather wet or put floatant on it, it will still retain its shape while the chicken feather won't, so don't substitute another material for wild bird feathers.

To continue the story, by our second season in business this spent caddis pattern had really gained a lot of local popularity. One evening that season, Ernie Schwiebert and I walked across the road in front of the shop to fish the hatch. The trout were really working, but after a short time it became apparent that they were selectively taking about a size 20 spent microcaddis.

Well, Ernie didn't have a single spent pattern so I gave him four Spent Partridge Caddis. He proceeded to hook and land a 23" rainbow and hook another bigger fish that I almost netted before it took off, spooling Ernie. He wrote an article about that adventure in *Sports Afield* around 1979. He named the fly, Sheralee's Speckled Sedge. The name didn't stick, but the popularity of the fly really took off from there.

Egg laying adult caddis are very important on the Henry's Fork and many other streams. One species may be hatching while another species or even the same species is laying eggs. My experience is that the trout get extremely selective on the spents. The key in identifying whether the fish are taking emerging or spent caddis is to watch the behavior of the take. When they are on emerging caddis, the takes are characteristically aggressive, often splashy. They just sip the spents.

For people who come over to the Henry's Fork in June for the Western Green Drake hatch, they will find that this pattern works well in the evening when the trout are selective on spent microcaddis. I tie them in sizes 12 through 22, but I find that size 16 and smaller are most effective.

By the way, good luck convincing your wife that she should tie flies and you should field test them. The Spent Partridge Caddis was the last time I got away with that routine.

SPENT PARTRIDGE CADDIS

HOOK:	Tiemco 100, Dai-Riki 305 or equivalent, sizes 12-22
THREAD:	8/0 olive, or color of natural
ABDOMEN:	Olive Antron blend dubbing, or color of natural
THORAX:	3-4 peacock herls
WING:	2 partridge or grouse back feathers
HACKLE:	One grizzly, one brown neck hackle

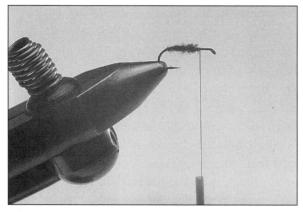

1. Dub a tapered body 2/3 the length of the hook shank.

2. Take 2 partridge or grouse feathers from the back of the skin. Tie the feathers with the curves facing away from each other which will make the wings flare right and left.

3. Attach one grizzly and one brown neck hackle on the near side of the hook.

4. Attach 3 or 4 peacock herls by their tips and wrap a thorax. Trim the ends and palmer the hackle through the thorax. Whip finish. Trim top and bottom of hackle flat.

5. Finished Spent Partridge Caddis from the side.

6. View from the front showing the splayed wings. These are easier for the angler to see than the old flat wing style of this fly.

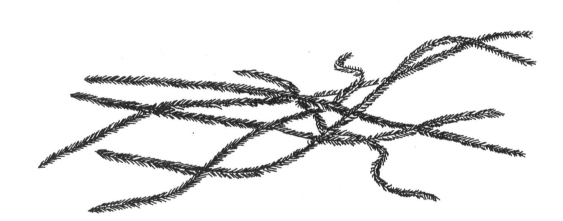

SPENT MIDGE

Mike Lawson

I like to get out fly fishing in the winter months as much, if not more than I do in the summer. There are no crowds and the fishing can be very good. It's a great cure for cabin fever.

Midges are a prime source of food for trout in the cold months of the year. One particular pattern I have used with good results when fishing during the winter is the Spent Midge. It does a good job of imitating midges which have become spent on the water from the cold air temperatures. Trout will sit in the eddies and on feed lines to sip them as they stack up.

The Spent Midge is an extension of the Spent Partridge Caddis. The key difference is that the wing is tied shorter and much more sparse on the Spent Midge. I like to use a partridge feather as the wing on this, and many other flies. I don't think there is any other material which will hold it's shape or natural shading as well as partridge or grouse feathers will. The body can be either gray or olive dubbing, but a wrapped quill body also works well. Next tie in the wing, make a couple of turns of grizzly hackle and finish the fly by clipping the bottom of the hackle flat. This is a cinch to tie.

The Spent Midge should not be considered to be just a winter pattern. Midges like cold water, that's why they are so numerous in high mountain lakes, spring creeks and tailwater fisheries. I have done really well with the Spent Midge on the spring creeks in Livingston, Montana. Another place it's been good is on Utah's Green River. It's probably not a pattern I use enough. Like everyone else, I have a Griffith's Gnat mindset when I see midges on the water. Fortunately, I do keep Spent Midges in my fly box. They have saved the day for me more than a few times.

SPENT MIDGE

HOOK:	Tiemco 100, Dai-Riki 305 or equivalent, sizes 16-22
THREAD:	8/0 olive
ABDOMEN:	Natural goose biot
UNDERWING:	Few strands of olive Z-lon
OVERWING:	2 light gray partridge back feathers
THORAX:	Olive Antron dubbing, Scintilla is an excellent choice

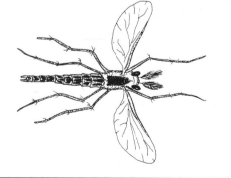

1. Tie in a goose biot at the rear of the fly and using hackle pliers wrap forward to the thorax. Overlap wraps slightly.

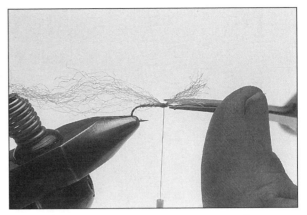

2. Tie the olive Z-lon in at the thorax to form an underwing. Trim front and rear. Should extend 1/2 hook length beyond the end of the hook.

3. Tie in the overwing of light gray partridge feathers just as you did for the wing in the Spent Partridge Caddis. Tie this not quite to the bend of the hook.

4. Dub a thorax and head. Whip finish.

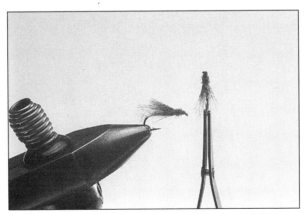

5. Side and bottom view of the finished Spent Midge.

TERRESTRIALS
& OTHER
TROUT FOOD

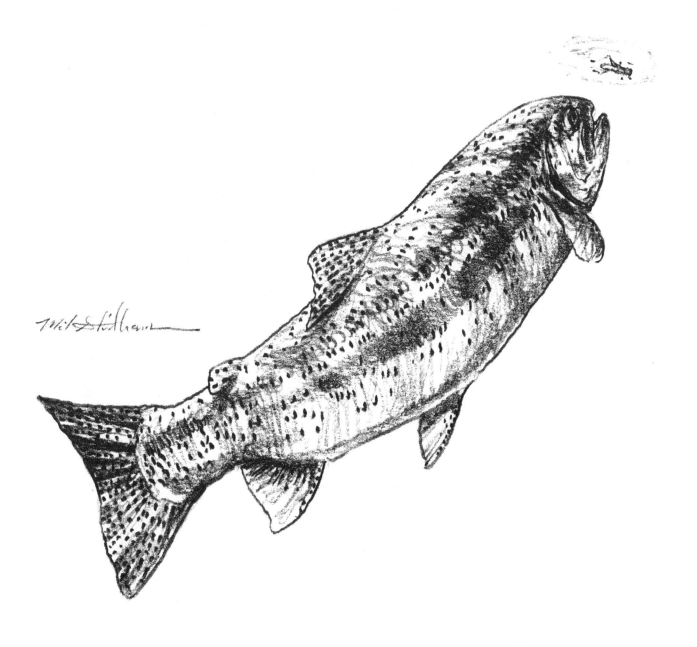

MUTANT NINJA CICADA

Emmett Heath

There is a very popular cicada hatch in the flora surrounding Utah's Green River below Flaming Gorge Dam. It occurs approximately May 15 through the end of June. This insect replaces the much missed stonefly, which is in such small numbers it is not even considered when hatches on the Green are discussed.

The cicada hatches in multi-year cycles making it a very vague insect to match. However, it has been a steady hatch on the Green for the past six years, and has caused a pilgrimage of anglers comparable to the angler following of the giant stoneflies of other large western rivers such as the Madison, South Fork and Henry's Fork.

There are many different patterns of cicada tied for the Green river. Some utilize clipped deer hair, while others use hackle in more traditional styles. It is basically up to the tier's needs or whims.

This particular tie comes from a long line of patterns used on the Green. The rubber legs come from the Madame-X. The foam for the body is just a material of the times, and along with the deer hair wing, it makes the fly very buoyant. The deer hair wing also provides a good silhouette. Hackle is used mainly to keep the bug stable and high in the water so that it's visible to the angler. The reason for the double legs is to give more wiggle to the fly.

It is hard to say who the inventor of the Mutant Ninja Cicada is because there were so many closely related ties evolving at the same time. Allan Woolley, Jeff Cox, Dennis Breer, Mark Forslund, Larry Tullis and myself, all guides on the Green, could claim a bit of it.

The Mutant Ninja Cicada makes an excellent attractor pattern for the remainder of the summer and fall. We have used it to imitate hoppers and crickets with a good deal of success.

MUTANT NINJA CICADA

HOOK:	Tiemco 2312 or equivalent, sizes 6-10
THREAD:	3/0 burnt orange monocord
BODY:	Black closed cell foam
UNDERWING:	Gold Krystal Flash
OVERWING:	Natural deer hair
LEGS:	Black or brown rubber legs, med size
HACKLE:	One or two grizzly neck or saddle feathers

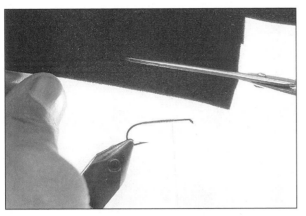

1. Wrap a thread base on the middle half of the hook shank then cut a piece of foam for the body.

2. Shape the foam with scissors then attach to the shank of the hook with tight thread wraps. Form a distinct indentation as shown.

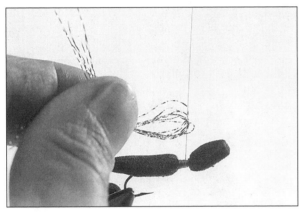

3. Loop strands of Krystal Flash around the thread as shown. This will be the underwing.

4. Cinch down the thread securing the Krystal Flash. Trim to the end of the body.

5. Select two unsplit pieces of rubber leg material for legs.

6. Place a right then a left pair of legs by looping the rubber around the thread just as you placed the Krystal Flash on top of the hook.

7. Tie in an overwing of deer hair, length to the end of the body. Do not overwrap the trimmed butts with thread (they will not pull out).

8. Select matching pair of neck hackles. Trim the fibers off the butts.

9. Tie in by the trimmed butts and wrap the hackle.

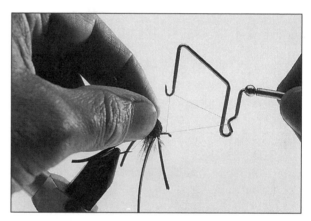

10. Whip finish in front of the foam.

11. Trim the right and left legs to desired length.

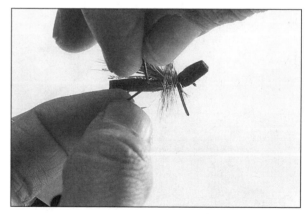

12. Split the pieces of rubber leg material. This will give two pairs of legs on the right and left side of the hook.

13. Trim the hackle flush on the bottom of the fly.

14. Side view of the finished Mutant Ninja Cicada.

15. Bottom view.

16. Top view.

CHERNOBYL ANT

Emmett Heath

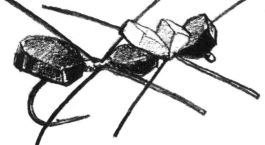

There is a giant cricket in Eastern Utah affectionately called the Mormon Cricket which migrates in very thick hordes. This huge cricket tries to cross rivers such as the Green, but in doing so becomes dormant due to the temperature change created by the cold water, and floats helplessly down river. It doesn't take too many of these to fill even a large brown trout's gullet, so you must hit it at the upstream end of the migration. Downstream, there will be no fish moving at all unless a Rolaid drifts past. The Chernobyl Ant's silhouette imitates this Stone Age looking cricket very nicely.

Much like the Mutant Ninja Cicada, the Chernobyl Ant makes a very good attractor. An advantage of this pattern to a guide fly tier is that the synthetic materials used to tie this fly make it durable, very buoyant, inexpensive and quick to tie. When a guide gets off the water, he doesn't have a lot of time to devote to fly tying. He must tie his stack of flies for the next morning as quickly and easily as possible. Quick and easy doesn't detract from the effectiveness of this pattern. During the late 1991 season on the Green River, the Chernobyl Ant was far and away the number one pattern for pulling fish.

I attribute the invention of this pattern to two Green River guides. First, Mark Forslund came up with the design. His pattern was called the Black Mamba. It was a very good fly in its own right, but it was hackled. Next, Allan Woolley took Mark's pattern and replaced the hackle with rubber legs to create a lifelike wiggle. The finished Chernobyl Ant isn't pretty, but it is a real winner when it comes to catching trout.

CHERNOBYL ANT

HOOK:	Tiemco 2312 or equivalent, sizes 6-8
THREAD:	3/0 burnt orange monocord
BODY:	Black closed cell foam
LEGS:	Black med. size rubber legs
INDICATOR:	Yellow closed cell foam

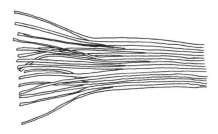

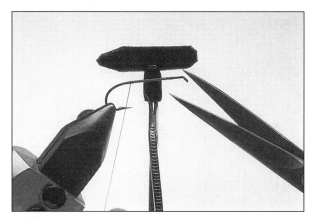

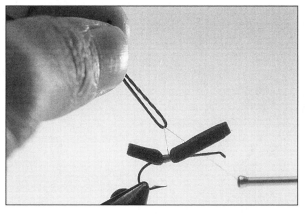

1. Wrap a base of thread on the hook and cut a piece of foam to size and shape for the body.

2. Tie in tightly with thread and form a distinct rear segment above the hook point.

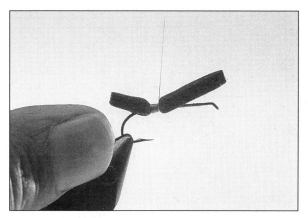

3. Loop a single piece of rubber leg material over the thread and secure to the far side of the hook. Repeat this process to the near side of the hook.

4. Top view of what the right and left pair of legs will look like when secured.

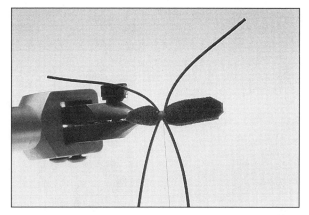

5. An underside view showing ' X-ing ' of the thread under the middle section of the 3 segment body. This gives durability to the fly.

6. Repeat the thread segmentation in the forward section of the fly and tie in the legs the same as in the rear section.

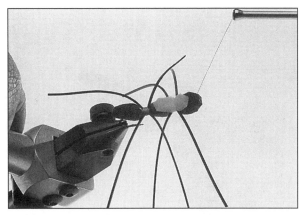

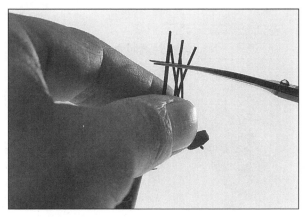

7. Tie in a piece of colored foam on top of the forward segment as a visual aid. Whip finish in front of the foam.

8. Cut the legs to length all at one time.

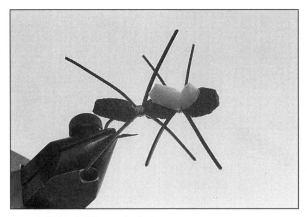

9. Finished Chernobyl Ant.

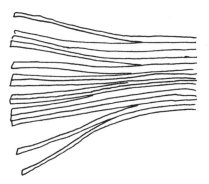

BEAR'S BROWN NO-HACKLE FLYING ANT

Bear McKinney

This is another of the many fly patterns in this book which were developed by observing the natural characteristics of an insect and then incorporating some of the new fly tying materials to imitate those characteristics.

Bear McKinney, a Jackson Hole fishing guide and fly tier, said that over the years the only pattern that he ever had semi-consistent luck using as an imitation of flying ants was Rene Harrop's Cinnamon Ant. In the summer of 1991 he noted that trout which had been fished over were selective to the point of being shy of Rene's ant. After capturing and examining a few live specimens, Bear concluded that standard ant patterns didn't come close to imitating the natural.

The Antron used for both the wing and legs is a key to the success of Bear's ant pattern. The wing is sparse enough to allow light to both penetrate and scatter. The legs are also tied sparse and give the impression of real legs as well as acting like outriggers to stabilize the fly on the water. Finally, the use of fine dubbing material makes it easy to create well proportioned body segments.

Compare the profile of Bear's ant to other ant patterns which you might have. I think you will find both the structure and function of Bear's Brown No-Hackle Flying Ant to be far superior. It will not only give you the edge in fishing to selective trout but you will be able to see the wing of the fly and the sipping take.

Bear's ant can be tied in black, cinnamon or any other color to match the various colors of naturals.

NOTE: Bear's ant probably crosses over as both an emerging and spent insect form of mayflies, caddis and midges.

BEAR'S BROWN NO-HACKLE FLYING ANT

HOOK:	Dai-Riki 305 or equivalent, sizes 12-20
THREAD:	8/0 dark brown
BODY:	Very fine poly dubbing, rust or dark brown color
WING:	Fluorescent white Antron Body Wool
LEGS:	Dark brown Antron Body Wool

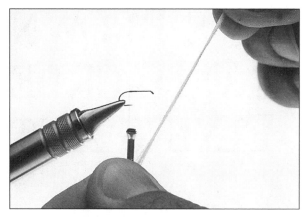

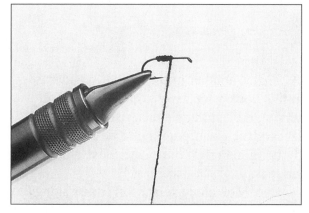

1. Attach the thread to the hook and form an underbody as shown. Stretch the Antron wing material. Do the same with the Antron leg material and set both aside.

2. Apply dubbing to thread and wrap back and forth to form an abdominal ball.

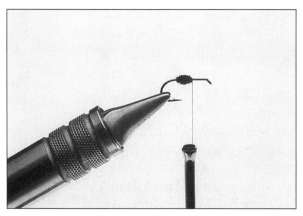

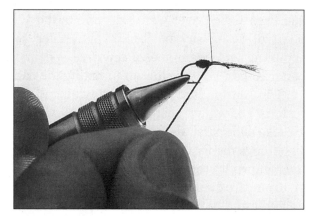

3. Shows size and position of the dubbed abdominal ball on the hook.

4. Wet about 10 fibers of the Antron leg material with saliva and attach to the top of the hook with a couple of loose wraps.

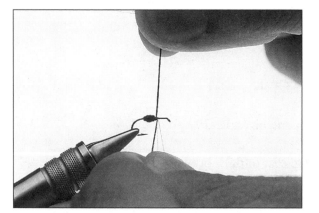

5. Use your fingers to twist the material to the bottom of the hook shank.

6. Figure eight with thread to secure the legs to the bottom of the hook.

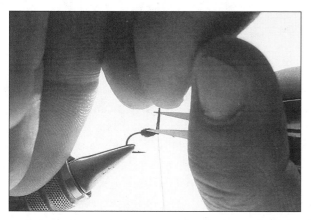

7. Pull the leg material and clip to about the length of the abdominal body part.

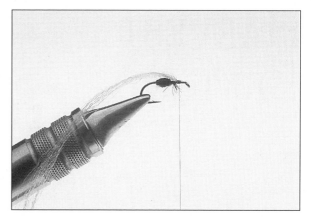

8. Tie in a sparse amount of the white Antron wing material just in front of the legs and splay over the abdomen.

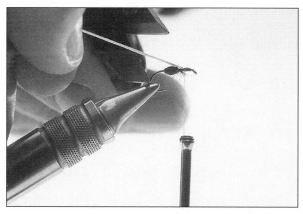

9. Pull the wing material back and cut at the butt of the hook.

10. Shows the position where you will dub a thorax. It is slightly smaller than the abdominal segment. Whip finish.

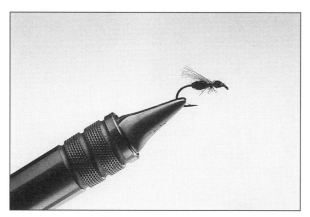

11. Finished Bear's No-Hackle Ant.

HARVEST BEETLE

Don Storms

The Harvest Beetle was first tied in the autumn of '91 on the banks of the Delaware River just below Hancock, NY. Farmers cutting their fields chased beetles and other insects into the river. After watching this manmade hatch for about an hour, I noticed that trout were starting to work the surface. I caught a couple of beetles and went back to my car to tie a few. When I had completed a couple of my new beetle knock-offs, it was time to test them. I didn't pick a particular trout, but rather cast in the general direction of some working fish to see what would happen. Happen it did! About ten feet into my first drift, I was solidly connected to a fat, sixteen-inch, wild Delaware River rainbow. Oh, what a feeling!

The Harvest Beetle can be tied to fit your applications. The back can be tied with deer hair, elk hair or foam. The body color can be varied, and dubbing can be used instead of floss. Don't be afraid to experiment.

HARVEST BEETLE

HOOK:	Mustad 94833, Dai-Riki 300 or equivalent, sizes 14-18
THREAD:	6/0 tan
BODY:	Yellow floss, or fine poly dubbing
LEGS:	Tips or deer hair used for back
BACK:	Brown dyed deer hair, or to match naturals

1. Wrap the thread from the center of the hook shank to just above the barb then wrap back to the center. Select a bunch of deer hair to be stacked.

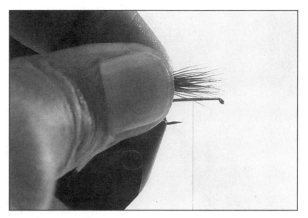

2. The tips of the stacked deer hair should just touch the eye of the hook.

3. Secure the hair at mid hook shank and wrap back to the above the barb as shown.

4. Divide the hair tips equally to each side to form the legs. Use your fingers and figure eight thread wraps to accomplish this.

5. Dub or floss an underbody as shown.

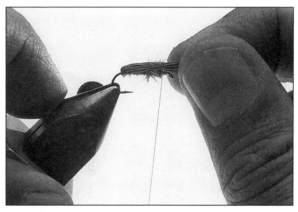

6. Pull the butts of the deer hair forward over the legs and to the head.

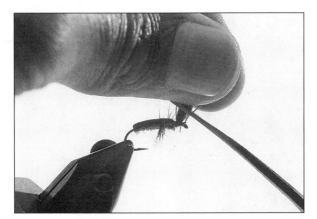

7. Secure with thread wraps and trim the butts leaving a hair head. Whip finish.

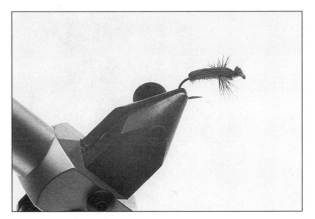

8. Finished Harvest Beetle.

HAIR BEETLE

Jack Dennis

It was an early September morning on the Henry's Fork. The dissipating mist revealed three trumpeter swans lazily swimming across the river. Tucked in a little indentation on the far bank, a slow rise caught my attention. Once again, a slow rise appeared at the same spot. This looked like a good size fish.

My friend, Mike Lawson, better known as "the Dean of the Henry's Fork," leaned over and philosophically said, "I know this fish. I've tried to get him before but failed."

"Mike," I said, "it's a new day. Let's give him a go."

We were on the Henry's Fork that day to film a segment of our video, *Tying and Fishing Caddisflies*. Mike reached into his vest and pulled out a fly box. "If I am lucky enough to hook this fish, it will be great for the cameras. He's a big boy. He feeds in this little back water and it's tough to get a drag free float to him. One mistake and he's history."

The first fly out of his fly box was a Black Caddis, next a Partridge Caddis, then a Pale Morning Dun... Mike even tried a size 24 Griffith's Gnat. An hour had passed and we had plenty of video footage of flies floating on the water while that fish went on rising. Mike looked at me in disgust, then looked at the camera and said, "Shut that thing off for a second. Jack, if you want to have a good picture of a fish running and jumping on film, you better let me pull out my secret fly box."

At this point, having a fish on camera, regardless of what it was caught on would be great. Out came the secret fly box and Mike pulled out a dark black fly with a little red tuft.

"This fly works every time," Mike said. I peered at it and said, "That's a beetle!" "That's right, Jack," Mike replied. "Everybody thinks that the Henry's Fork is a match the hatch stream. Well, every time I can't match the hatch, I put this beetle on and it does the job for me. In fact, it might be my favorite fly on this stream."

Mike had a good drift on his first cast and as the beetle floated over that big rainbow, there was a gentle sip and the hook-up. The water exploded as the trout headed downstream. Mike leaned over and without an ounce of excitement in his voice said, "Maybe I should have brought my five weight today instead of my four weight."

I never really paid much attention to a beetle until that day. Since that time, I have worked on a variety of different beetle patterns. I have found one that I feel is easy to tie and will work as well as the one Mike used on the Henry's Fork. I call it the Hair Beetle for lack of a better name. This pattern is not totally unique, but rather a combination of parts from other patterns. I think it is the best of all worlds.

Tie the Hair Beetle and give it a try. Be careful not to overdress it. Try to fish it in the surface film, but if it does sink, let it continue its drift. You'll be surprised how many fish will take it that way. I am sure you will be as amazed as I have been at how consistent this pattern works. It may become your secret favorite fly too.

HAIR BEETLE

HOOK:	Dai-Riki 300 or equivalent, sizes 10-16
THREAD:	6/0 black
BODY:	Dark Scintilla or other fine poly dubbing
BACK:	Dyed black deer hair
RIBBING:	2 strands pearl Krystal Flash
LEGS:	Root beer or other dark Krystal Flash
INDICATOR:	Orange Glo Bug yarn

1. Lay down an underbody of thread on the hook shank. Select, stack and clean a clump of deer hair.

2. Tie in the deer hair by the butts at mid shank and at the top of the hook as shown.

3. Attach 2 strands of pearl Krystal Flash for ribbing. Note: it is difficult to see in the photo due to its translucence.

4. Dub the thread for the underbody.

5. After dubbing the body 2/3 of the way up the shank, rib with Krystal Flash.

6. Select strands of root beer or dark colored Krystal Flash for the legs.

7. Attach the legs in front of the body with figure eight thread wraps.

8. Pull back the legs and make even thread wraps in front of them.

9. Pull the hair over the back of the body and legs.

10. Secure with several thread wraps in front of the legs.

11. Trim the butts. Can whip finish in front of the trimmed butts here if you don't put on a visual aid (step 13).

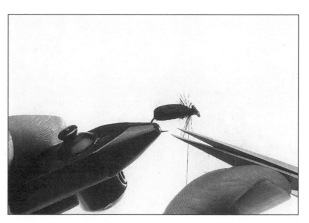

12. Trim the Krystal Flash legs to length.

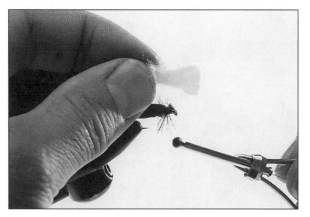

13. Place a short piece of Glo Bug Yarn on top of the leg area and tie in. This is a visual aid.

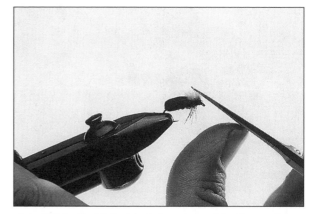

14. Whip finish behind the eye and in front of the head. Trim the visual aid short.

15. Finished Hair Beetle.

JAY-DAVE'S HOPPER

Jay Buchner

This fly originated on the Snake River in Jackson Hole during the mid-1970's. The addition of legs to an already popular Dave's Hopper came about on a pleasant day of fishing with my friend, Dave Whitlock. During that fun day of fly fishing show-and-tell, an unnamed hopper pattern with legs turned a few heads. Enough heads were turned that Dave and I went from the river to the tying vise, and before dinner, the legs had become an addition to the original Dave's Hopper.

The new fly, Jay-Dave's Hopper was fished the next day on the Snake and was an immediate hit with the trout and critics. Dave and I like it too. Since the 70's Dave and I have spent quite a few angling days enjoying each others company, especially during the hopper season.

JAY-DAVE'S HOPPER

HOOK:	Mustad 9671, Dai-Riki 730 or equivalent, sizes 2-14
THREAD:	3/0 yellow monocord for body, black A monocord for head
TAIL:	Red dyed deer hair
BODY:	Pale or bright yellow poly yarn
RIBBING:	Brown hackle
LEGS:	Golden pheasant center tail feather
UNDERWING:	Deer body hair
OVERWING:	Wild turkey tail feather
COLLAR:	Deer body hair

1. Put the stem of a golden pheasant tail feather in the vise and select out a small bunch of fibers. Do not cut fibers off the feather.

2. Hold the tips of the fibers with the thumb and index finger of the left hand and place the open jaws of the forceps on the underside of the fibers.

3. Draw the tips under the jaws of the forceps as shown. The tips in your left fingers will come behind the fibers over the jaws to set up a simple overhand knot.

4. Bring these tips over the top and place into the open jaw tips. Gently grasp the tips with the jaws as shown.

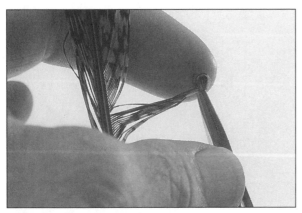

5. Pull the tips through the overhand knot with the forceps.

6. Form a knot as shown. This is the joint of the leg. Repeat this procedure on the opposite side of the stem for the matching leg.

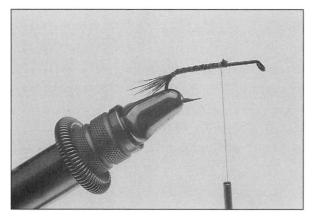

7. Secure a small stacked bunch of red dyed deer hair about mid shank and cover with thread wraps to and slightly around the bend as shown.

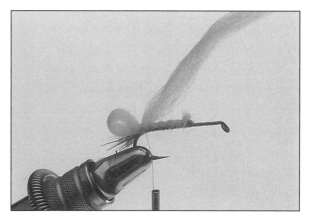

8. Tie in a piece of yellow yarn at mid shank and make a loop at the butt as shown.

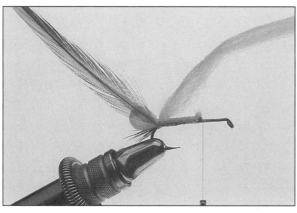

9. Tie in a brown saddle feather at the near side of the hook at the butt. This will be the palmered ribbing.

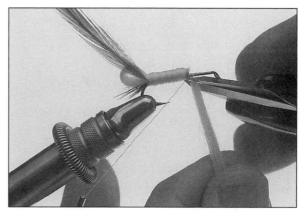

10. Wrap the yarn forward, tie off and trim. Note the abrupt untapered end of the yarn body.

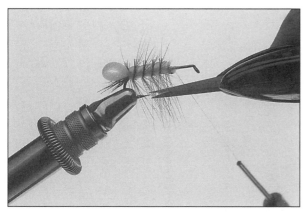

11. Palmer the hackle through the yarn body and trim short on the top and sides, and a gape length on the bottom.

12. Tie in the hair underwing on top of the yarn body, not in front of it. The length of this is to the end of the looped butt.

13. Make a few loose wraps of thread back over top of the underwing to draw it downward as shown.

14. Cut a segment from a turkey tail feather that has been treated with a plastic spray for the overwing and cut the butt into a ' V ' shape as shown.

15. Secure the turkey overwing with the ' V ' shaped end facing back to and on top of the underwing, not in front of it.

16. After trimming the forward tip of the overwing, tie in the right and left legs slightly to each side of the overwing.

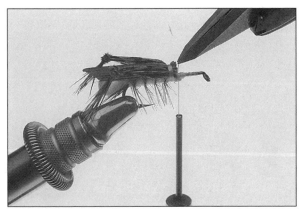

17. Trim the butt of the legs then bring the thread in front of the leg tie in point. Whip finish the 3/0 thread at this point. Glue this spot with Flexament.

18. Attach the A mono thread. Measure the cleaned, stacked deer hair collar for length as shown.

19. Surround the hook shank by sliding the deer hair bunch over it. Make a couple of loose wraps then make tighter wraps which will flare and secure the hair.

20. Place a bunch of cleaned deer hair with the tips and butts trimmed over the top of the hook. Note the thread position.

21. Make a couple of loose wraps of thread then let the hair spin as you tighten the next wraps. Whip finish in front of the head.

22. Put the fly in the jaws of forceps and begin trimming the head flat on the bottom.

23. Trim the sides and top of the hair head to shape making a slight angle inward (apparent in step 24). Be sure to leave the deer hair tip collar.

24. Finished Jay-Dave's Hopper from the side and bottom .

FLAT CREEK HOPPER

Ralph Headrick

This outstanding grasshopper pattern is another of the highly effective creations of Jackson Hole guide, Ralph Headrick. It was developed out of frustration with the ineffectiveness of other patterns, through meticulous observation of naturals, and with plenty of trial and error at Ralph's tying bench.

Ralph tells the story of the Flat Creek Hopper this way:

"One warm October day about seven or eight years ago I drove up to Yellowstone Park to fish the Firehole River. The thermal effects of the geyser basin which the Firehole flows through, coupled with the warm days of summer, increases water temperatures beyond a trout's tolerance. With the shorter day length and frosty nights of autumn, the water cools and the river can really turn on. If the day doesn't get too bright or warm, you can have a lot of fun fishing emergers and small drys. But, on those bright warm days of Indian summer, when there are no hatches, there is plenty of grasshopper activity to interest the trout. Many anglers are of the belief that the frost of late August and early September kills terrestrials. This is far from the truth. Grasshoppers, ants and beetles are still around for the fish to see well into October.

"On the October day I visited the Firehole it was warm and dry. There were little grasshoppers everywhere and the trout were really on them. Continuous perfect hopper presentations resulted in continuous refusals. Although the fish would drift up from the slow moving holds along the grassy banks to examine and bump my imitations, they wouldn't take them. This was not the first time that this happened to me with grasshoppers, but I was determined it would be my last.

"Before leaving, I collected some of the natural hoppers in a jar so that I could examine them at home and try to tie a perfect knockoff. After close examination I realized that the legs and low profile of the insect in the water were the dominant features. Something I hadn't noticed before was how smooth the underbodies were, with only light serrations. Lastly, the naturals always floated right side up, which is something that commercial patterns don't always do. I spent all winter tying variations and dunking them into the jar with the naturals. By the summer after my autumn Firehole experience, the Flat Creek Hopper was ready to field test.

"I named the fly after Flat Creek, my favorite fishery. Flat Creek cutts see plenty of real and unreal grasshoppers, and by the second week of the season they are tough to fool. The Flat Creek Hopper has performed with consistency from day one.

"My favorite color is natural elk, but light green, yellow, or rust can also work. I don't know why, but some days a red body is real hot. If you tie it all black, it is a good cricket imitation."

Ralph feels that although his hopper pattern will work anywhere, it is particularly deadly on slow flat water where the trout get a good look at the fly. He admits to still using Jay-Dave's Hopper for heavy water.

This is a popular pattern in Jackson Hole but difficult to get hold of as Ralph no longer commercially ties them. However, the cult following of the Flat Creek Hopper has learned that this fly is probably the easiest to tie and the most durable grasshopper pattern around.

FLAT CREEK HOPPER

HOOK:	Tiemco 5263, Dai-Riki 710 or equivalent, sizes 6-12
THREAD:	Yellow size A monocord, or color to match natural
BODY:	Gold dyed elk hair, or to match natural
LEGS:	Golden pheasant tail feather fibers (10-12 per leg)
WING:	Turkey tail feather sprayed with clear acrylic
HEAD:	Natural deer hair

1. Mark your scissor blades with a pencil to equal the distance from the eye to the bend of the hook.

2. Attach the thread at the front of the hook as shown. Cut the tips off of cleaned, stacked elk hair.

3. Place the elk hair bunch over thread wraps with the butts forward and hold in place with about 6 loose thread wraps.

4. Roll the hair to the bottom of the hook with your fingers and secure with tight thread wraps. Cover with thread wraps to the hook point.

5. Attach the deer hair head with tips forward according to marked length on the scissor blades (step 1). Keep this hair on top of the hook.

6. Flare the deer hair with tight wraps of thread and trim butts but do not wrap over them.

7. Pull back the elk hair to form the body. Do not let go of the hair. Begin to rib back with the thread to 1/3 back from the eye.

8. Continue ribbing back with the thread to the position as shown to behind the hook then rib forward with thread wraps.

9. Trim the elk hair at the bend of the hook behind the end of the ribbing. Glue the end with Flexament.

10. Prepare a ' V ' shaped turkey tail overwing just as you did in the Jay-Dave's Hopper. Page 216, steps 14-15.

11. Tie in the overwing at the 1/3 point. The tip of the 'V' is just to the butt of the fly. Trim the tag end.

12. Prepare a pair of legs just as you did in the Jay-Dave's Hopper. Page 214, steps 1-6.

13. Tie the leg on the far side of the hook then on the near side at the same 1/3 point as shown.

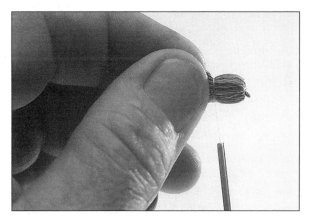

14. Pull the deer hair back to form a head and secure at the 1/3 point.

15. Whip finish at the 1/3 point. Note the flared tips of the deer hair collar.

16. The finished Flat Creek Hopper from the side and bottom.

LARRY'S SWIMMING LEECH

Larry Walker

In the early 80's I was one of a large group of Denverites to take over a shoreline of North Delaney Lake in Northern Colorado for a weekend. Many of us were purist stream fishermen who had recently discovered how much fun it was to get in a float tube and chase trout around a pond.

I had recently become aware of the importance of leeches to trout, especially in lakes like North Delaney. Most of the imitations we had were of the Woolly Bugger variety. They were effective but I wanted a soft fur leech pattern. I had already made my original Dubbit tool so I was into loop-dubbing everything. A soft fur leech was an automatic for the Dubbit.

One day I sat around camp working on a new leech pattern while the rest of the group was on the water. I had a concept of a leech pattern which would move in the water. If the patterns being used at the time weren't being stripped or trolled they would die in the water.

I discovered that a slight forward weighting of the hook shank would help. When I add lead to a pattern, I wrap it around the hook shank. This causes the fly to roll around to some degree.

I pondered the problem of how to lead the hook. I needed to redistribute the weight somehow. If I would strip-lead the bottom I would lose the profile. I discovered that if I wrapped the hook shank with lead, then placed my forefinger under the eye of the hook and my thumbnail about one-third of the way back on top of the hook, that I could bend the front of the fly up slightly. The weight distribution was at a lower point and the fly rode in the water the way I wanted it to. A second result, which was a total surprise to me was the fact that this leech pattern would swim. It had a realistic movement which other leech patterns had only if they were stripped or trolled.

My favorite colors for the Swimming Leech are black, olive and rust brown. Sometimes I'll put black tails on the olive or rust leeches, or do a dark head by placing some black fur in the dubbing loop last. If I blend fur for a body, I like to add a pinch of clear Antron. This can be deadly.

I get rave reports on the Swimming Leech from friends who have used it on everything from mountain lakes and spring creeks, to large rivers. One friend really cleaned up using it on Nevada's Pyramid Lake. If you are using the Swimming Leech in a river, hold it in the current and it will move back and forth. Don't try this unless you are using heavy leader material because the fish really slam it. I think you will find the Swimming Leech to be a fun fly to tie and especially fun to fish.

LARRY'S SWIMMING LEECH

HOOK:	Tiemco 5263, Dai-Riki 710 or equivalent, sizes 4-10
THREAD:	3/0 black monocord or color to match
LEAD:	.025
UNDERBODY:	4 strand wool yarn/ Dave's Flexament
TAIL:	Rabbit fur cut from the skin, use the same color as the body; marabou can be substituted
TAIL FLASH:	2 strands Krystal Flash or Flashabou
BODY:	Rabbit fur cut from the hide; black, rust and olive are common colors

1. Heavily weight the center of the fly over a thread base as shown.

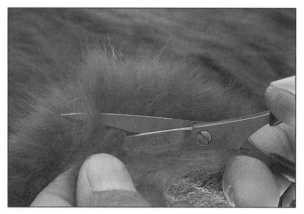

2. Cut a medium bunch of fur from a rabbit hide to be used for the tail.

3. Attach the tail behind the lead as shown. The tail should not fold down over the bend of the hook.

4. Loop a piece of Flashabou or Krystal Flash around the thread and secure. This will leave one strand on each side of the tail.

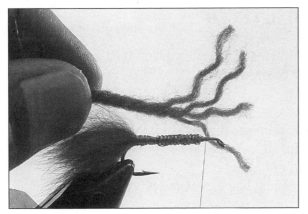

5. Four strand wool yarn will be used as an underbody.

6. Tie the wool yarn in on the right and left side of the lead and to the tail. The yarn is on the sides only of the fly. Whip finish.

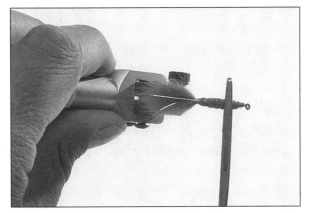

7. Flatten the body with smooth jawed forceps or pliers making it wider than it is thick.

8. Liberally coat with Dave's Flexament. Stage tie a number of these through this step.

9. Reattach thread. Precut 4 or 5 bunches of rabbit fur and place where readily available. After forming a loop with the Dubbit, insert bunches into the loop with butts to one side.

10. With all the fur tips lined up, trim the butts close to the thread as shown. It helps to pinch the base of the thread loop with the left thumb and index finger.

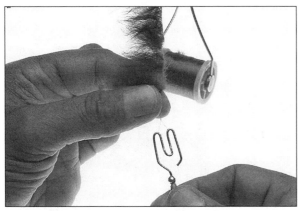

11. Rotate the Dubbit 6 or 7 times while pinching the thread together. The Dubbit can now be spun without throwing the material out of the loop.

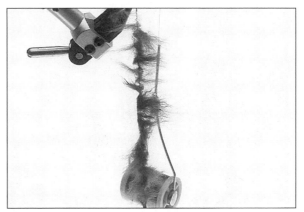

12. Notice that the fur starts to turn over in the loop as you begin to spin the Dubbit.

13. Shown here; the spun loop which will be used to wrap the body.

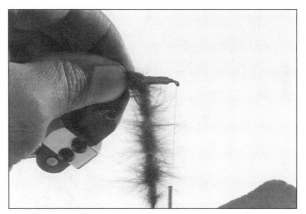

14. Wrap the fur loop forward pulling back the fur of the previous wrap each time so you don't wrap over the top of it.

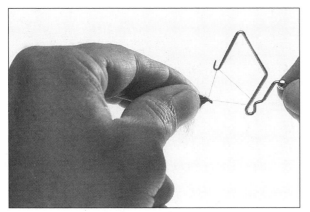

15. After wrapping the fur body to the eye of the hook, whip finish.

16. Pick out the fur body with the bodkin creating an even body.

17. Trim the fur on the top and bottom flat. This now gives a wide flat body.

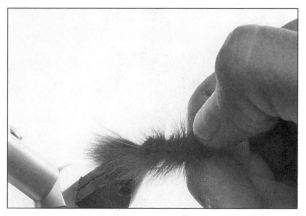

18. With the fly in the vise, put the index finger under the hook, the thumb on top of the hook, and bend the front of the hook up.

19. The finished Larry's Swimming Leech.

CROSS-CUT SCUD

Jack Dennis

Scuds are not insects, but rather crustaceans. In the quality habitat they share, scuds comprise an abundant high energy food source for trout. To give you an idea of what a diet of scuds does to a trout's physique, think of the results of force feeding rice to sumo wrestlers. Anglers who have seen the shape of trout from rivers like the Green and Bighorn can quickly relate to this analogy.

Color is a key consideration when you tie and fish scud patterns. Trout see scuds in colors which include tan, pink, gray, olive and orange. Lighter colors, such as tan and pink, occur when scuds are molting their outer shell. As a new outer shell hardens, it darkens to a protective color which blends into the aquatic environment. Trout can probably see the lighter colored molting scuds easier than non-molting ones. Dead scuds turn orange and fish won't have any trouble seeing them.

Another consideration when you tie and fish scuds is size. They can range in size from microscopic to jumbo within the same fishery, so tie them as small as you care to go or as large as a size four. There is an interesting article on lake flies by John Shewey in the July/August, 1992 issue of *American Angler*. In it, he describes scuds large enough to batter dip and deep fry. Don't be afraid to try a little trial and error with size and color when you fish scuds.

A variety of natural and synthetic materials can be used to tie scuds. Angora goat hair or Scintilla dubbing material both work well. Scintilla used with Larry Walker's cross cut dubbing technique gives the scud a very translucent body. Dubbing on the finished fly can be picked out with a dubbing teaser to create lifelike ventral appendages. A Renzetti rotary vise is an added luxury when tying them.

The scud is usually taken on the dead drift when fished in moving water. However, you can get action at the end of the drift when the fly swings; so fish it out. If you are fishing two flies, the scud is a good dropper. In lakes or very slow deep holes like you see on Utah's Green River, use either a floating or sinking line to cover the depth of the water you are fishing. Retrieve the scud with a four or five inch twitch to mimic the natural's darting movements.

As a final tip, try fishing scuds at dawn, dusk, on an overcast day or in the dark. Scuds have a very negative reaction to light and are much more active during poor light conditions. The exception to this would be in a tailwater where a sudden release of water can flush scuds from their shelter. As a rule of thumb, the more available a food source, the more selective the trout will be to that food source. Keep this in mind next time you are fishing a tailwater and you suddenly see the water level rise.

CROSS-CUT SCUD

HOOK:	Dai-Riki 135, Tiemco 2457, 2487 or equivalent, sizes 6-22
THREAD:	8/0 olive or color to match natural
TAIL:	Webby base of dyed grizzly hackle feather
BODY:	Olive/brown Scintilla or other sparkle blend
SHELL:	Plastic cut from a Ziploc bag
RIBBING:	Fine gold wire
ANTENNAE:	Webby base of dyed grizzly hackle feather

1. After laying down an underbody of thread on the hook shank from the eye to above the barb, select fibers from a webby grizzly hackle.

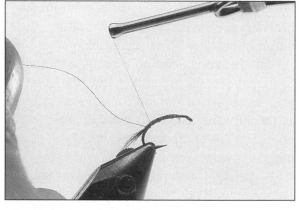

2. Tie in the grizzly fibers as a tail just above the barb of the hook. Tie in wire ribbing at the same point.

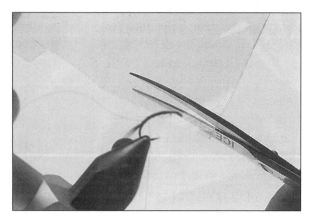

3. Cut a piece of plastic from a Ziploc bag to be used for the back.

4. Tie in the plastic strip at the same point as the tail and wire ribbing.

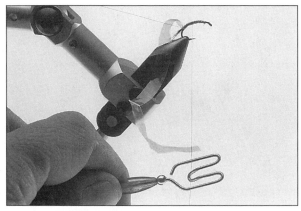

5. Slide the thread into the Dubbit as shown.

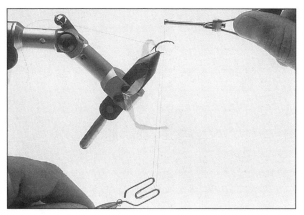

6. Form a loop with the thread.

7. Close off the loop by dropping the thread over the top of the loop.

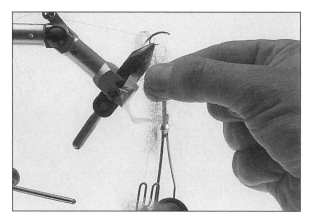

8. Slide dubbing up into the loop and pinch with your fingers to give an even row of fibers.

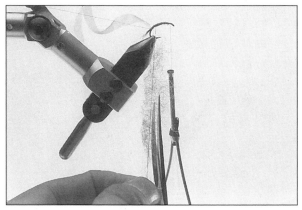

9. Cross cut the right and left side of the dubbing close to the thread as shown.

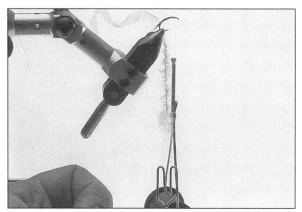

10. Give the Dubbit a spin which will form a fuzzy chenille as shown.

11. Attach the webby grizzly hackle fibers to form the antennae just as you did with the tail.

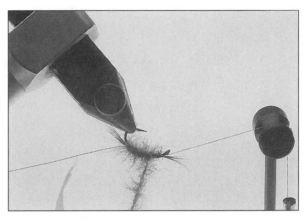

12. Wrap the dubbed loop forward to form the body. A rotary vise for this step makes this easier.

13. Pull the plastic strip over to form a back shell and secure with thread wraps and trim the tag end.

14. Rib the wire to the eye of the hook. Tie off and trim. Whip finish under the antennae.

15. The finished Cross-Cut Scud. The fly on the right shows the translucent profile when the fly is wet.

SNAKE RIVER MUDDLER

Jay Buchner

My unending interest in finding good uses for great materials that aren't getting a lot of press coverage has led to some interesting creations. Several years ago I became attracted to grizzly marabou feathers because they looked great but were not being used in many patterns. The possibilities seemed limitless. A large number of experiments and test patterns ensued. Some of the experimental patterns showed promise, but needed modification. Soon I had a fly box full of experiments and test flies. One application was for streamers. The grizzly marabou did a good job of simulating the barring on small trout and some minnows. The test patterns of the streamer were fairly numerous.

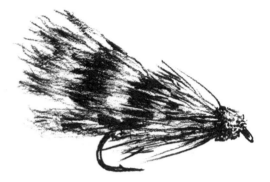

One fall day I was float fishing the Snake with Joe Burke. We were anchored and looking for a fly that might get a little more attention than what we had been using. Joe spotted my box of unnamed test flies. With a shopper's eye, he made a selection and asked, "What's this called? I've never seen a Muddler like this before." My normal reply in these situations is, "I don't know what it's called; it's just an experiment." Joe tied the experiment to his leader and proved he knew a good fly when he saw one. The trout agreed and Joe later decided it should be called the Snake River Muddler. It has not only become his favorite Muddler pattern, but it is also the only Muddler pattern he ties and fishes.

SNAKE RIVER MUDDLER

HOOK:	Mustad 79580, Dai-Riki 700 or equivalent, sizes 4-10
THREAD:	3/0 black for body, A monocord for head
TAIL:	Tip of yellow dyed grizzly marabou feather
BODY:	Same feather as tail wrapped on hook
UNDERWING:	Fox squirrel tail
OVERWING:	Two yellow dyed grizzly marabou feathers
COLLAR:	Deer body hair
HEAD:	Deer body hair

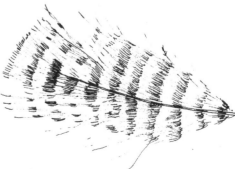

1. Attach the tip of a dyed grizzly marabou feather to form the tail. Do not trim off the remaining feather.

2. Wrap the remaining marabou feather around the thread as shown.

3. Wrap the marabou wound thread 2/3 up the hook shank. Trim the tag end.

4. Tie in a sparse underwing of squirrel tail.

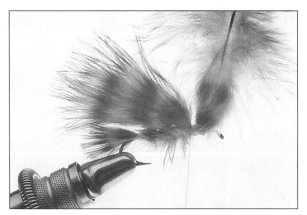

5. Tie in an overwing of two tips of dyed grizzly marabou feathers. Note the length past the tail.

6. Lift the marabou wing and make a couple of thread wraps beneath it which will lock it in place. Whip finish here. Can stage tie through this point.

7. Attach a monocord thread. Make a collar by sliding the deer hair into the hook in the same fashion used in the Jay-Dave's Hopper. Note the length. Page 217, step 19.

8. Start with a few loose wraps then flare the hair with a few progressively tighter wraps.

9. On larger sized flies you may need to fill the head out by flaring an additional hair bunch in front of the first. Whip finish in front of the head.

10. Trim the head to shape.

11. The finished Snake River Muddler.

DOUBLE BUNNY

Scott Sanchez

The idea for the Double Bunny came to me about five years ago when I was fishing in Belize. My friend John Hanlon and I had a great time catching barracuda. We found that the most effective flies were Jack Dennis' Kiwi Muddler and a long Fishair cuda fly. The Kiwis' rabbit fur wing and the cuda fly's Fishair both have an oscillating movement when stripped. In additon, the cuda fly has large eyes which are a triggering mechanism for predatory fish.

On subsequent saltwater fishing trips, I observed that predatory fish would often seem non-aggressive next to baitfish. However, if one of those baitfish acted differently, then the predator would nail it.

Trout are also predatory, and I fish for them more often than I do barracuda. "Big fish eat little fish" is a truism. However, the little fish aren't always as small as you expect. I've caught too many trout with sculpins in their mouths that dwarfed a size 2 streamer and also had 16" trout try to eat 8 to 10 inch trout off my leader.

What I needed was a fly to trigger these predatory responses. I wanted a big fly that gave me greater consistency than Deceiver style streamers.

Most fish have two dominant colors, a light belly color and a dark back color. Common belly colors for fish in trout streams are white, light gray, tan, yellow, gold and silver. Common back colors are olive, brown, tan and various shades of gray.

Baitfish in trout streams range from 3/4" to 8" in length. The 3/4" to 3" size range is covered well by streamers such as Kiwis, Zonkers and Wooly Buggers. That leaves a large void in the over 3" streamer category. Flies in the larger range are the ones most likely to tempt "Mr. Big".

When I considered shape, I observed that most trout and baitfish are about four to five times as long as they are deep. They taper back at the head and then are roughly the same depth back to the tail. Baitfish, with the exception of sculpins, are usually much longer than deep. I have also noticed that minnows and trout fry have proportionally larger eyes than bigger fish. Lefty Kreh, among others, has noted that predatory fish attack the eye of a baitfish.

The action of a fish was the final thing I needed to mimic. Fish swim by moving their whole body. Fins push the water, while the back and forth movement of the body muscles power the fins. Additionally, the body movements of an injured fish are erratic.

With all these factors in mind, I concluded that a good big fish streamer should have a dark back and light belly; be in the 3" to 8" size range; have a tapered body and conspicuously large eyes; and the entire fly front, back and middle must be able to move.

Light and dark strips of rabbit fur laminated together sounded pretty good to me and made the dual coloration that I needed. Gluing on round pieces of reflective tape made realistic eyes. The fact that it is tied on two hooks that are tied together with mono gave it the movement I wanted.

The Double Bunny in color combinations of olive and white or olive and yellow have been deadly on cutthroat and mackinaw trout. I am sure that they would work for other freshwater species, and when tied on a stainless steel hook, they would work well on barracuda, sharks and jacks.

A great deal of thought and experimentation went into the creation of the Double Bunny. It, however, was worth it as it does exactly what I had envisioned it doing. It looks absolutely alive in the water, even when dead drifting. Best of all, it catches big fish.

DOUBLE BUNNY

HOOK:	Tiemco 8089 Bass Bug Hook or equivalent, sizes 2-6
LEAD:	.035
BODY:	Zonker strips or rabbit hides glued together with Barge cement to interface dark color on top, lighter color on bottom
LATERAL LINES:	Copper Flashabou
EYES:	Reflective sign tape and black vinyl adhesive tape

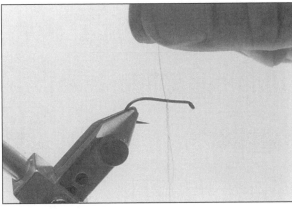

1. Use mono to snell the trailer hook if you plan to use a trailer. See the illustrations on page 238, or the book, *Practical Fishing Knots II,* by Mark Sosin and Lefty Kreh.

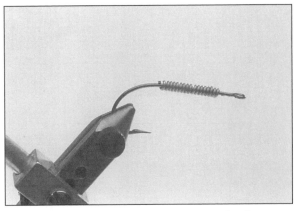

2. Weight the primary hook with heavy lead wraps as shown.

3. Tie on the mono from the trailer hook at the rear of the lead and cover with thread wraps to the eye. You can double the mono over and rewrap if desired.

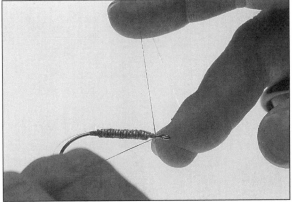

4. Whip finish the thread and cut. You may wish to glue the lead at this point.

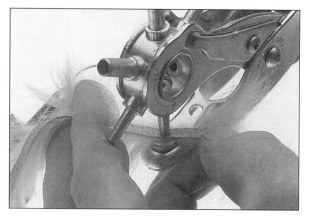

5. Using a leather punch put a hole in the light color rabbit strip as shown.

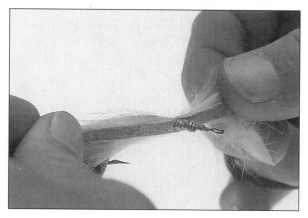

6. Slide the rabbit strip over the eye of the hook.

7. Reattach the thread and pull the light color rabbit strip to the back of the hook.

8. Pull the hide side up along the bottom of the hook shank and tie down at the eye of the hook.

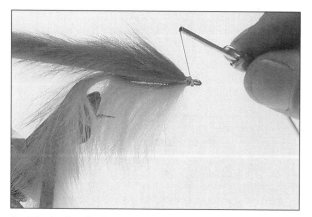

9. Tie in the dark colored rabbit strip on top of the hook with the fur side up.

10. Use liberal amounts of contact cement in the following steps.

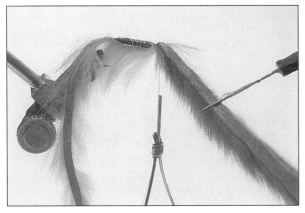

11. Apply cement to the hide side of both strips. A bodkin works best to apply cement without getting it in the hair.

12. Put a liberal amount of cement on the leaded hook shank.

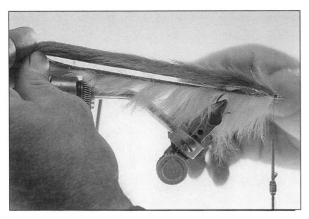

13. Pull the two hide sides evenly together as shown to cement them together. Push them together with your fingertips.

14. Tie in the copper Flashabou across the hook ' X-ing ' it with the thread then pulling it back and tying over it to form a right and left lateral line.

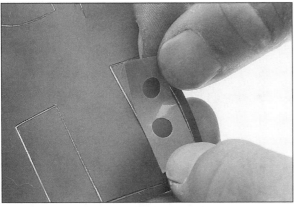

15. After punching two holes out of reflective sign tape, stick it to the black vinyl adhesive tape as shown.

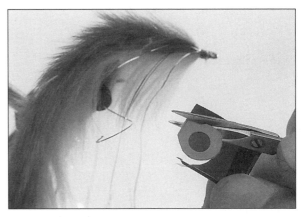

16. Cut around the two overlaid pieces of tape forming a pair of eyes.

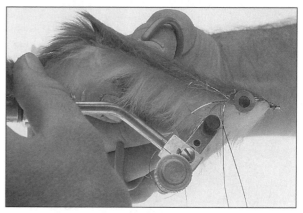

17. Glue the eyes to the right and left sides of the fly over top of the Flashabou and fur with contact cement.

18. Cut the glued strip of rabbit hide to length by sliding the scissors in from the side so as not to cut the fur. This tapers the tail.

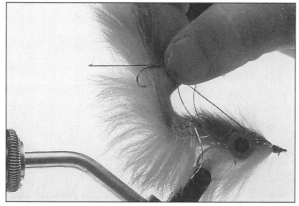

19. Puncture the rabbit hide with the sharp trailer hook from the bottom to the top. Trailer hook is positioned upside down.

20. The Finished Double Bunny.

Snelling the trailer hook.

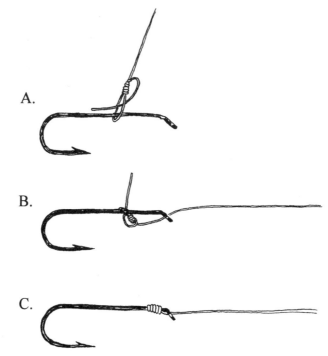

A.

B.

C.

ATTRACTORS

PEPPERONI YUK BUG

Jack Dennis

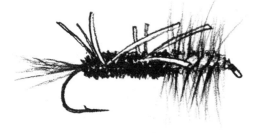

In all my years of fishing, probably the best wet fly fisherman I have seen is my friend, Robbie Garrett. He was also one of the best fly fishing guides around until he formed a company to make luggage for Patagonia. As a guide, Robbie was a fine boatman and a great coach. He never let me get away with a sloppy cast or wrong retrieve and always forced the best out of my fishing skills. I always told him he was the Bobby Knight of fly fishing.

Everything Robbie does, he does with intensity. He has always said that the key to fly fishing is concentration. Robbie is a master at choosing the right retrieve for the right fly and situation. Sometimes he will dead drift the fly; other times he will interrupt the dead drift by pumping the fly and sometimes he will jig it.

When it comes to designing, tying and fishing rubber leg flies, Robbie has no peer. I remember introducing him to rubber leg flies in the early 70's. I gave him a black Girdle Bug and he instantly fell in love with the pattern. Until that point, his favorite fly was a Muddler Minnow, tied and fished the Garrett way, of course.

A few years later, another rubber leg fly came out of Montana called the Yuk Bug. It had great popularity on Montana's famous rivers: the Big Hole, Beaverhead and Jefferson. Robbie modified the Yuk Bug and concocted his Pepperoni Yuk Bug. He felt that of all rubber leg patterns, that "the Pep" as he calls it, best represents a stonefly. It catches fish whether stoneflies are out or not. If stoneflies are out, it's magic.

I wrote about the Pepperoni Yuk Bug in an article for *Fly Fisherman Magazine* in the mid-80's. Soon, fly shops in the area were getting requests for this mystery fly. It has become a standard pattern for those who appreciate the main value of rubber legs: movement in the water, which gives the fly a lifelike appearance. Whether the rubber legs annoy or attract the fish, no one knows.

Robbie insists that the Pepperoni Yuk Bug be fished dead drift, with the angler raising and lowering the rod tip occasionally to make the legs move in and out. It should not be fished with long strips like a streamer, because this smashes the legs up against the body, rendering the fly useless. Short strips work as long as there is a pause for the fly to drift as in "the Yuk Bug wiggle".

Most of the time, the Pepperoni Yuk Bug works best when fished on a dry line with a leader no longer than eight feet. Tie the fly on a weighted hook and put extra weight on the leader if needed to sink it quickly. It works well for big browns and also on panfish; so give "the Pep" a try.

PEPPERONI YUK BUG

HOOK:	Dai-Riki 700C or equivalent, sizes 4-10
THREAD:	3/0 black monocord
LEAD:	.020 or heavier
TAIL:	Red squirrel tail
LEGS:	Large white rubber legs
ABDOMEN:	Med or large black chenille, depending on hook size
THORAX:	Med or large orange chenille, depending on hook size
HACKLE:	Brown saddle hackle

1. Lead the hook as shown and cover with wraps of thread. Tie in the tail behind the lead 1 1/2 hook gapes in length. Cement the lead.

2. Tie in the black chenille at the tail tie in point.

3. Cut two unseparated pieces of rubber leg material. Securing with figure eights, attach the rear set of legs just behind the lead and the front set at mid-shank.

4. Wrap the black chenille to just in front of the forward set of legs.

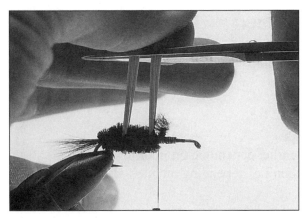

5. Pull the legs up together and cut all at once to desired length.

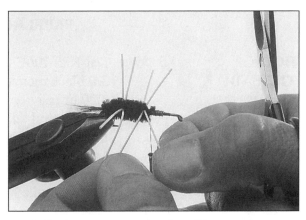

6. Split the unseparated pairs of legs as shown.

7. Tie in the orange chenille just in front of the forward set of legs.

.

8. Tie in the hackle feather with dull side toward you at the same place as the orange chenille.

9. Wrap the orange chenille to the eye of the hook and trim. Palmer the hackle forward and trim. Whip finish.

10. The finished Pepperoni Yuk Bug.

TURCK TARANTULA

Guy Turck

This fly was originated by Jackson Hole fishing guide Guy Turck. In the summer of 1990, while guiding for High Country Flies, Guy's clients were having reasonably good luck using the Madame-X. With the omniscience common only to guides, Guy recognized some of the shortfalls of this pattern. First of all, it did not always float well. He solved this by using a spun deer hair head. Secondly, most commercially tied Madame-X's have a thread body. He felt this was too sparse and replaced it with a more life-like tapered, dubbed body. Lastly, he noticed how much difficulty clients had seeing the Madame-X. For visibility, he added a calf tail wing. By August he had developed but not named his pattern.

Part of the fly name came from one of Guy's fishing clients. When he handed his client one of his new flies to try the man questioned, "What is this, a tarantula?"

"I thought it sounded good," Guy said. "By adding my name, I hoped to get enough fly orders to keep busy during the winter months."

Only one month after developing the Turck Tarantula, Guy offered the fly to George Anderson to use on the first day of the 1990 Jackson Hole One Fly. By the end of day one, George was far ahead of the rest of the field. Joan Wulff, George's fishing partner on day one, was one of the many in line on the morning of day two to get a Turck Tarantula. Their results for that day were all spectacular, but not enough to overcome George whose two days of "Tarantulizing" the trout earned him the championship.

Guy fishes the Tarantula dead drift until he feels it's in the fish's window, then he twitches it. He explains:

"This is when I get most of the action. In big fast water I just drift the fly and let the movement of the water wiggle the legs. At the end of the drift, if nothing happens, I swing the fly in the current, pull it under and pump retrieve it back wet."

This fly can be tied in various colors to match specialized hatches such as big salmonflies and golden stoneflies. And yes, Guy is staying busy in the winter months tying the alliteratively named Turck Tarantula. They are in great demand at local fly shops.

TURCK TARANTULA

HOOK:	Dai-Riki 710 or equivalent, sizes 4-12
THREAD:	3/0 unwaxed tan or to match color of head
TAIL:	Amherst pheasant tippet
BODY:	Hare's mask
UNDERWING:	White calf tail
OVERWING:	Pearl Krystal Flash
COLLAR:	Deer body hair
LEGS:	White or brown med. rubber
HEAD:	Deer body hair

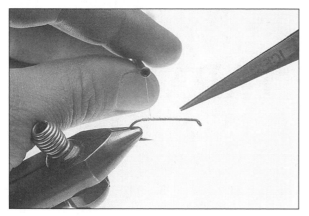

1. Lay an underbody of thread where the head will be and spiral thread to the point of the hook.

2. Above the barb tie in Amherst pheasant fibers a hook gape in length. Can get three tails from this one feather if selected as shown.

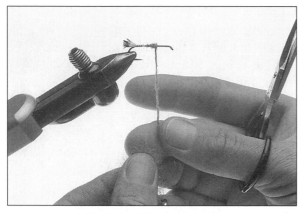

3. Use sparsely dubbed thread to dub from the tail to 1/3 back from the eye.

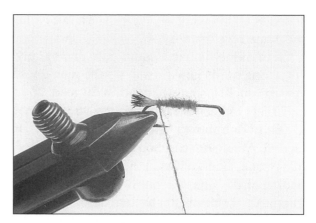

4. Wrap the dubbed thread back and forth creating a forward taper.

5. Finished tapered body.

6. Prepare the calftail wing by first pulling out the long hairs by the tips.

7. Remove the short base hairs with a toothbrush.

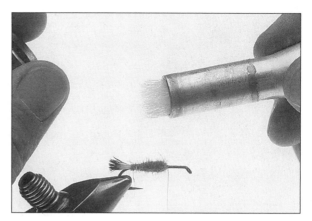

8. Stack the tips of the calf tail with the hair stacker.

9. Measure and then attach the calf tail underwing at the front of the dubbing. Length, to the tip of the tail.

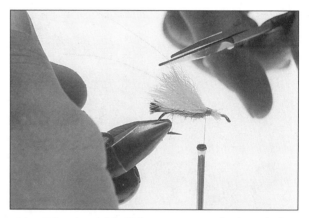

10. Trim the calf tail butts at an angle then tie in one piece of Krystal Flash on each side as an overwing. Trim to underwing length.

11. Prep deer hair for collar same as calf tail. Place it on top of the hook with the tips extending to the barb.

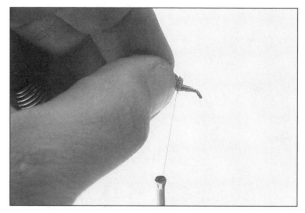

12. Tie deer hair in with 2 loose thread wraps and two tight wraps to flare 180 degrees and secure. Do not wrap over the trimmed butts.

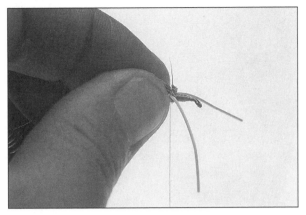

13. Attach a strand of rubber leg material to the far and then the near side of the hook. This should be kept long to make it easier to work with the head later.

14. Note that the legs are tied in only at the collar. You can whip finish and stage tie to here if you wish.

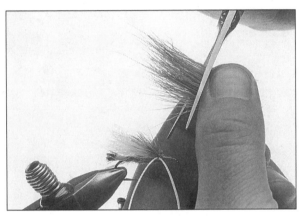

15. Reattach thread if stage tying. Prepare the deer hair for the head by clipping the tips of the cleaned hair.

16. Center the shank of the hook in the bundle of hair.

17. Slide the hair into place as shown. Do not extend the bundle as far as the hair collar tips.

18. Make 2 loose thread wraps then flare the hair by cinching it down with 3 more tight wraps.

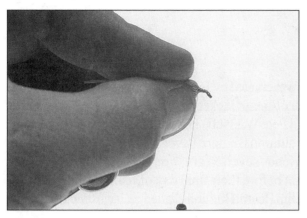

19. Pull back the hair with your fingers and make a couple of thread wraps in front of it. Repeat steps 16 - 18 for a fuller head on larger flies.

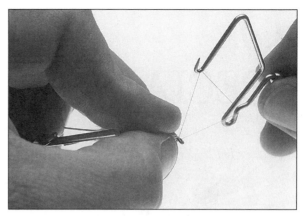

20. Pull back all the hair and whip finish behind the eye as shown.

21. Trim the head starting on the bottom first.

22. Cut the top, left and right sides as a triangle, smaller in the front and larger towards the collar. Take care not to cut the rubber legs in this step.

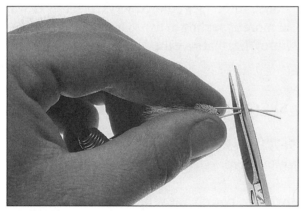

23. Trim the rubber legs to desired length.

24. The finished Turck Tarantula from the side and front.

J.J. SPECIAL

·Jimmy Jones

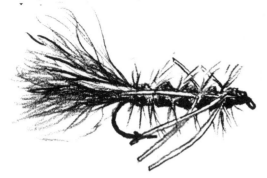

This fly was created by Jimmy Jones who owns and operates High Country Flies in Jackson Hole. "The Special" was named by his friend Pete Wiswell. The development of the fly can be traced to an autumn Bighorn River fishing trip made by Jimmy and a few friends seven years ago.

The night before their final day of fishing was filled with merriment, Jim Beam, Bud and challenge. It was decided that for the last day, everyone would tie on one fly and fish with that fly, and that fly only. Jimmy created the J.J. Special from table scraps left by other tiers. Marabou came from a Bighorn Special, chenille and rubber legs from a brown Yuk Bug, and Krystal Flash from a copper bodied Rabbit Matuka. Jimmy describes that final morning:

"The weather had turned cold while the prevailing wind drove the snow at acute angles to the water. It was impossible to keep your rod guides free of ice. My fishing buddies did modest at best with their flies. However, the table-scrap creation, the J.J. Special creamed 'em."

In subsequent years the J.J. Special has caught fish everywhere it has been used. "Ask Paul Bruun what he thinks about it. Bear McKinney used it in New Mexico and caught smallmouth bass on it. It has a cult following," Jimmy says. Who would question a following that included Bruun and Bear?

Jimmy says he likes to fish this fly with a slow pump retrieve. He says Pete Wiswell keeps his rod tip high and skims the surface with the fly and has very good results.

This is a fly that is worth tying. It has some very interesting tying techniques and proportions that can be applied to other flies you tie. Here are some examples you should take note of:

1) The short, stiff saddle hackle wound directly behind and in front of the rubber legs gives support and limits the range of movement of the legs. 2) The tail length with its lateral line of yellow marabou is a key. 3) The importance of copper colored Krystal Flash is way overlooked by most tiers. It seems to be far more appealing to fish than gold or silver.

Tie some J.J. Specials; these are the kind of flies that save the day for you when nothing else is working.

J.J. SPECIAL

HOOK:	Mustad 9672, Dai-Riki 710 or equivalent, sizes 4-8
THREAD:	3/0 black monocord
LEAD:	.025
TAIL:	Tip of brown marabou plume, yellow marabou on each side
LEGS:	Yellow or white size med. or large rubber legs
BODY:	Brown med. size chenille
HACKLE:	Grizzly saddle hackle
LATERAL LINE:	6 strands of copper Krystal Flash or Flashabou

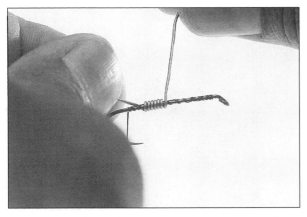

1. Lead the fly over a thread base from the point of the hook to 1/4 back from the eye.

2. Tie the tip of a brown marabou plume in for the tail. The length is the same as the hook.

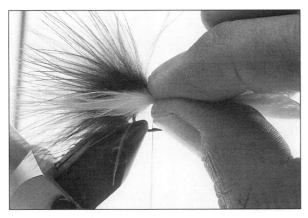

3. Attach the yellow marabou with fibers sparse and shorter on each side of the brown marabou tail.

4. Note: All the material tie in points are behind the lead.

5. Attach black chenille to the far side of the hook and the saddle hackle to the near side of the hook. The dull side of the hackle is toward you.

6. Wrap the chenille 1/3 up the hook shank. Loop an unseparated pair of rubber legs around the thread then tie in underneath the body.

7. Start to wrap the chenille through the legs as shown.

8. Wrap the chenille another 1/3 up the hook shank.

9. Attach another pair of rubber legs in the same manner.

10. Wrap the chenille the final 1/3 forward. Tie off and trim.

11. Separate the rubber legs as shown.

12. Loop 6 strands of copper Krystal Flash under the eye then secure with thread.

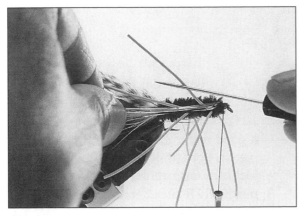

13. Pull the copper Krystal Flash between the rubber legs and along the tail on each side to form a lateral line.

14. Holding the Krystal Flash in place as shown, palmer the saddle hackle forward. Be sure to make a turn right behind and in front of each set of rubber legs.

15. After whip finishing the fly, clip the Krystal Flash strands the length of the marabou.

16. Clip the legs to length.

17. The finished J.J. Special.

Black Legged Waterwalker

Bruce E. James

The idea for this fly came from experimentation with a pattern we often use in Jackson Hole called the Madame-X, and it is a good one to tie while you're tying that pattern. For a while I've been toying with the idea of an unsinkable fly, thinking of how to make a fly float better in rough water. I had just bought some ensolite foam (a material they make life jackets from) the day before and was busy tying Madames for the upcoming season. While the standard Madame-X is a great pattern, I've had some trouble keeping it up in rough water. Looking at the newly purchased package of gray ensolite foam on my fly tying desk I thought, "why not", and began to experiment. The result was a fly that surprised me with its fishability.

The most exciting venture was when some regular clients of mine, Meredith and Susan came up for a few days to do some serious fishing. Since Meredith always outfishes Susan, I thought I'd give her the new pattern to try in hopes that it would help. The day started out nice, but became very windy and overcast. We came to a big pool that I knew held some good fish. Susan threw the Waterwalker into the top of the pool and immediately had a strike. After a battle with both the fish and the wind, which was blowing the boat around, she landed a nice cutthroat about 17 inches. I figured the commotion would put down any other fish, but had Susan make another cast anyway. She dropped the fly slightly downstream and instantly had another nice fish on. She continued using the Waterwalker for as long as my supply lasted, catching fish after fish. I was astounded with the results.

This is a great pattern to experiment with. There are a variety of colors of ensolite foam available which you can cover, if you choose to, with different dubbings. Dyed elk makes the most durable head and collar, but other hairs can be used. A pink strike indicator on the top is a nice option for gray days. You could also vary the color of the legs and add a tail if you wish. Experiment, that's what makes fly tying a pastime that has fascinated me for over thirty years.

BLACK LEGGED WATERWALKER

HOOK:	Mustad 94831, Tiemco 5212 or equivalent, sizes 6-10
THREAD:	6/0 black for body, 3/0 black for head
UNDERBODY:	Black or gray ensolite foam
BODY:	Black dubbing
LEGS:	Large black rubber legs
HEAD:	Elk hair tied bullet style
COLLAR:	Elk hair
INDICATOR:	Fluorescent egg yarn
WING (OPTIONAL):	White calf tail
MISC:	Slow drying cement such as Dave's Flexament

1. Cut a strip of black closed cell foam about 1/8 inch accross and 3 inches long. Tie this in with tight thread wraps about 1/3 back from the eye.

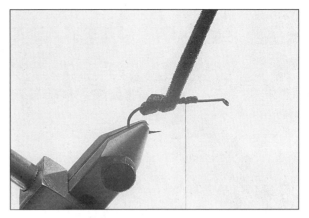

2. Wrap the foam forward to the 1/3 tie in point.

3. Apply a coat of Flexament to foam body.

4. Dub a body over the cemented body while still tacky. Do not pull tightly on the thread which would compress the body.

5. Make a thread base and tie in a calf tail wing, where the body ends. Cement this area.

6. Stack and clean a small bunch of elk hair. Tie in, tips forward, 360 degrees around the hook. Wrap tightly with thread to the eye and back to the calf tail.

7. Pull the elk hair back over the hair and thread base making a bullet head. Secure at the base of the wing with thread.

8. Tie in 2 pieces of black rubber legs loosely on top.

9. Position them to each side then tighten the thread wraps which will secure them in place. If a visual aid is desired, tie it in on top between the rubber legs. Whip finish and glue.

10. The finished Black Legged Waterwalker.

AIRHEAD

Gary LaFontaine

I can't think of any one fly that has been more fun for us than the Airhead. It has also been a great surprise too. We worked on this pattern with the idea of tying a concoction that would fail in our underwater testing phase. Why did we think it would fail? We used a type of foam that really diffuses light. Although a little diffusion is good, it was our premise that a lot of diffusion would be bad. The material, on patterns such as the Mess and the Halo Emerger, worked very well, but on those creations the foam provided an aura, an edge, over the body. We were really going to blast the light on the Airhead.

Tory Stosich was underwater the first time we tested the Airhead. It took a fish quickly enough and soon caught another trout. We were on good water, where most flies performed well, but the success of this strange attractor surprised the observers on the shore. Tory didn't even wait for the end of the fifteen minute diving period. He popped up to the surface to tell us, "Not only are they taking it, but they are coming a long, long way for it."

Many people, who fish with the Airhead, write and call with stories about it. One of my friends, Joe Burke, uses it frequently in the Jackson Hole area and has some terrific insights into the fly. Joe says:

"When you first tied the Airhead for me, I thought you were pulling my leg. It wasn't until I used it that I found out that you weren't joking. I have had clients, who were terrible casters, use it because they could at least see it on the water. More often than not, the fly wouldn't drift dead, but would swing and pull under. The trout would go nuts, and the clients would think they had mastered the art of fly fishing. As a guide, there is nothing better than seeing your clients overflow with that excitement.

"My favorite body color is gold, but at the end of last season I used some peacock herl and red floss to tie a variation I called the Royal Airhead. The Snake River cutthroats loved it. I have had remarkable success using the Airhead on small meadow streams. I put a lead shot at the leader knot and fish the fly across and downstream. I then strip it back under the cut bank. The takes are fierce."

The Airhead is an unpredictable fly, which is part of its charm. Sometimes it fails because the fish get too excited and slap at or jump over it. In the low light conditions of late evening they will sip it like a natural insect. It also works well for sunfish, perch, crappie and white bass. At all times it moves trout a long way.

AIRHEAD

HOOK:	Dai-Riki 300 or equivalent, sizes 8-16
THREAD:	8/0 yellow or color to match body
BODY:	Any color sparkle dubbing; Scintilla #31 golden is good
WING:	Deer body hair
HEAD:	6 strips of clear closed cell foam

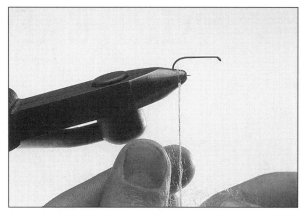

1. Sparsely dub thread at the rear of the fly.

2. Dub a slightly tapered abdomen to the middle of the hook as shown.

3. Tie in a sparse flared deer hair wing over the abdomen.

4. Trim the butts of the hair and sparsely dub the thread for the thorax of the fly.

5. After dubbing the thorax, begin adding the foam spokes behind the eye of the fly. They point forward.

6. Repeat to cover the head of the fly with 5 to 6 foam spokes. Wrap the thread back to 1/3 from the eye.

7. Pull all the spokes back together to form a bullet head and whip finish the thread at the 1/3 point.

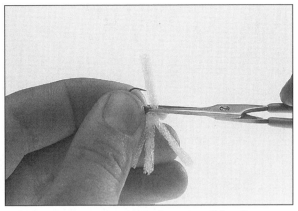

8. Trim the spoke off the bottom of the fly.

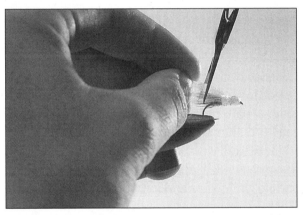

9. The spokes on the side are trimmed short and the spokes on the top are trimmed long all at once.

10. The finished Airhead.

MOHAWK

Gary LaFontaine

The Mohawk is actually my daughter Heather's pattern. She tied it a number of years ago, but it has only recently become commercially available through Umpqua Feather Merchants. She doesn't like me to tie it in public because I'm not the neatest fly tier in the world, so she thinks that my version is a little ragged.

Is the Mohawk different than other flies? Well, I do love the history of fly fishing and I have never seen anything like it. The spun deer hair body on most patterns is egg-shaped. On the Mohawk, the deer hair body is cut in a radical 'V'. The shape of the hair body inspired the fly's name (from the Mohawk haircut).

The 'V-shape' of this pattern creates a distinct float because the fly is top heavy. When it lands on the water, the weight of the deer hair pushes most of the mass underwater. That doesn't happen with other hair patterns, such as the Rat-Faced MacDougal or the Goddard Caddis.

The Mohawk serves as both an imitator and an attractor. It may be taken by the trout as a beetle, an insect they see daily for a good portion of the season. The angler can use it with confidence anytime he would use a grasshopper pattern.

In October, 1992 I was on Utah's Green River filming a video with Jack Dennis and our friend, Emmett Heath. Emmett was on the side of a hill with Steve Horton and our film crew, Mark Rohde and Joe Burke. Emmett and Steve could easily spot the fish in the gin clear water. They would tell me where the fish were feeding, while Mark and Joe would follow the action with the camera. This was quite a team effort.

I was using one of Jack's favorite two-fly techniques. With this method a small nymph hangs as a dropper about 10 inches off the eye of a dry fly. It was apparent to everyone that the trout were nymphing not far below the surface. Typically, when trout are nymphing like this, they focus at a certain level and will not come up for any dry fly. I was using the Mohawk as the dry indicator fly to illustrate Jack's technique for the video.

The Mohawk totally messed up the filming. The fish would see it, streak right past the nymph, and nail the dry fly. We finally had to take the Mohawk off and replace it with a pattern that wasn't such a strong puller.

The rear, hair section of the Mohawk can be tied in any color. The front part of the deer or elk hair is always white, providing great visibility. The front hackle is oversized, not meant to float the fly but to simply dangle and wave the fibers under the surface. This fly can be either an imitator or an attractor, so be sure to have a variety of colors in your fly box.

MOHAWK

HOOK:	Dai-Riki 300 or equivalent, sizes 10-16
THREAD:	6/0 white or black
REAR BODY:	Green, orange or rust dyed deer hair or natural deer hair
FOREBODY:	White deer hair
HACKLE:	White or cream neck hackle, oversized X2

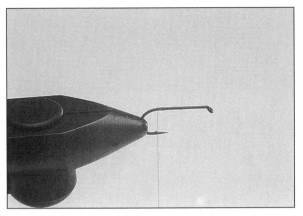

1. Attach thread at the rear of the hook shank.

2. Spin a segment of hair at the rear of the fly as shown.

3. Pack the spun hair and put a half hitch right in front of the hair. This prevents problems if the thread breaks.

4. Repeat the above procedure with another bunch of hair to cover 2/3 of the hook.

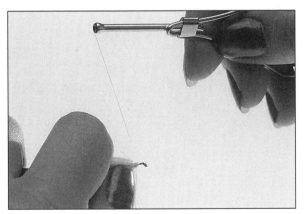

5. On the forward 1/3 spin a clump of white deer hair and whip finish in front of it.

6. Take the fly out of the vise. First trim the bottom but not flat. Next trim the right and left sides to form a ' V ' in the bottom.

7. Put the fly back in the vise. Pull all the hair up at once, tilt the scissors downward toward the rear and trim at an angle.

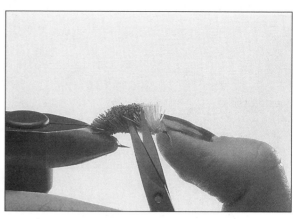

8. Trim out any renegade hairs.

9. Reattach the thread and tie in a oversized neck hackle. Make one or two hackle wraps, whip finish and glue.

10. The finished Mohawk.

CREATURE

Gary LaFontaine

Is the Creature an attractor or an imitator? Well, as the name implies, it does imitate a small creature, maybe a mouse or some other animal swimming in the water. It is designed to have action on the retrieve. Rabbit fur is tied over an underbody of foam, which provides flotation. Since the foam is never evenly distributed, the fly wobbles in the water. Add this wobble to the pulsation of the rabbit fur and the result is a very lifelike appearance.

This fly is a lot of fun to fish. Small trout bump it, but big fish slam it. I fished the Beaverhead in Montana when the river was producing a lot of big browns and rainbows. One evening I had four Creatures in a row broken off (on 0X tippet). The monsters came up and just wanted to kill it.

The Creature triggers a competitive spirit in trout. At times, two or more trout rush the fly, trying to smash it, engulf it and pull it down. This is very exciting surface fishing, so no one with a weak heart should even cast this fly.

CREATURE

HOOK:	Tiemco 7989 Dry Steelhead Hook or equivalent, sizes 2-8
THREAD:	3/0 black or brown monocord
UNDERBODY:	High density foam used for popper flies
TAIL:	Tag of shaved rabbit hide cut in a taper
OVERBODY:	Brown or gray rabbit strip
HEAD:	Rabbit fur cut from hide

1. Select a piece of high density foam used for popper flies.

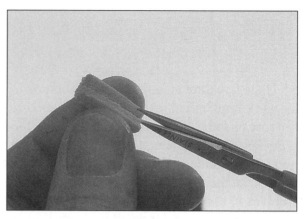

2. Cut to length then cut a seam down the center of the foam.

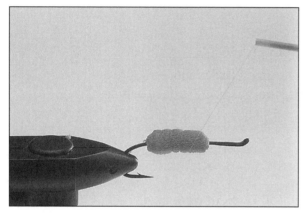

3. Secure to the hook shank from above the hook point to about 1/2 forward.

4. Wrap down with tight thread wraps.

5. Pull the fur off the tag end of the rabbit strip, tie in at the butt of the hook as shown and shape into a ' V '.

6. Wrap the strip of rabbit fur around and just forward of the foam.

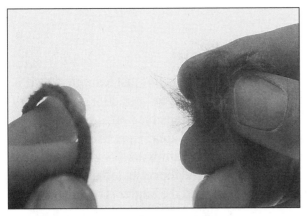

7. Pull some more rabbit fur from the hide to use as dubbing.

8. Loosely dub the thread as shown.

9. Wrap a dubbed thread head and whip finish.

10. The finished Creature.

DOUBLE WING

Gary LaFontaine

Actually, the Double Wing is not just a single fly. It is a series of flies based on a theory of attraction. The theory rests on the fact that color has intensity. And light varies with the season, time of day and the area. Here are examples:

If an angler is next to a stream with lots of green trees, the light is hitting the leaves and the reflected rays are green; or, when it is late in the day and the angler is on open water, with the sun setting, the light reaching the trout stream is mostly red and orange. The color of the ambient light reacts with the color of the fly to create intensity (or lack thereof).

When the Double Wing series was created, the idea was that color would be important in the puzzle of attraction, but would not be the dominant factor. However, the strength of color attraction, evident from both our fishing and underwater observations, turned out to be far more significant than we ever expected.

I was the guest on the Clark Fork River, below Missoula, filming an ESPN fishing show. That morning Mark Jones, one of the finest guides on that river said, "You know, attractors really don't work here."

I told him, "I have no choice. I have to put on the Double Wing for filming."

The fishing had started slowly that chilly Autumn morning, but Mark finally pulled the boat off the water to let us wade fish. "You might try the fly here," he said.

The host of the fishing show fished a riffle below me. He was using dry flies, but he was not getting any strikes. On my stretch of river there were two cameras set up waiting for me to start casting (now that is pressure). I was fishing the Double Wing where attractors weren't supposed to work; using it at a time when no one else was catching fish on a dry fly. But the Double Wing saved me again -- eight casts hooked five beautiful, bouncing rainbows. Of course, the host hasn't invited me back to do another show, but then that's Hollywood.

The Double Wing, no matter what the color variation, has a "hot spot" at the back of the fly. There is a stub tail of bright Sparkle Yarn, topped first by a wing of deer or elk hair and second by a wing of white calf tail. This prismatic layering captures and accentuates the ambient light.

DOUBLE WING

HOOK:	Dai-Riki 300 or equivalent, sizes 8-18
THREAD:	6/0 or 8/0 pale yellow green
TAIL:	2 strands of separated 4 strand sparkle yarn
TAG:	White 4 strand floss
REAR WING:	Green dyed elk or deer
FOREWING:	White calf tail hair
BODY:	Touch dubbed lime sparkle yarn
BODY HACKLE:	Olive dyed grizzly neck hackle
FORE HACKLE:	Grizzly neck hackle

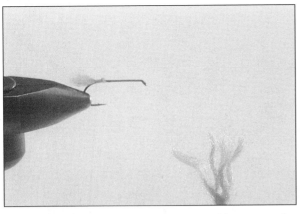

1. Comb out 2 strands of 4 strand sparkle yarn and tie in as a tail.

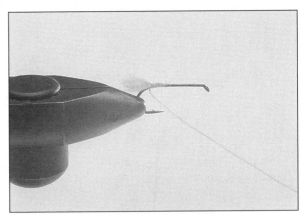

2. Tie in a piece of 4 strand floss for a tag.

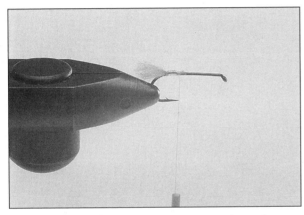

3. Wrap the tag from the butt of the tail to above the point of the hook.

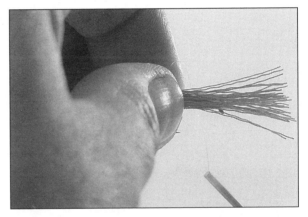

4. Tie in the cleaned, stacked dyed elk hair for the rear wing. Length should be just over the tail.

5. Tie in grizzly hackle feather to be used for palmering.

6. Touch dub the thread that has had tacky wax applied to it as was done in the Diving Caddis. Page 187, steps 1-2.

7. Dub a body slightly more bulky than the Diving Caddis to 1/3 back from the eye.

8. Palmer the hackle through the dubbing.

9. Trim the top palmered hackle.

10. Tie in the calf tail forewing which is slightly over the rear wing in length.

11. Tip to secure hair wing: Lift the wing forward, bring the thread and bobbin behind the wing as shown then go to step 12.

12. Drop the wing and make a few clockwise wraps around the hair and hook to lock the wing in place. Trim the butt ends of the calf tail.

13. Hackle the front of the fly and whip finish.

14. Finished Double Wing.

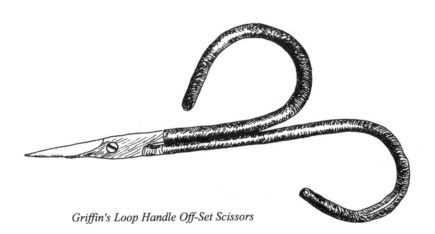

Griffin's Loop Handle Off-Set Scissors

CHUCK'S TRUDES

Chuck Stranahan

My interest in Trudes began with the enthusiasm of Ron Falk, an impeccably skilled Bitterroot Valley fly tier who tied for my shop in Northern California during the late seventies. "Try 'em. They're great!" he exhorted. I did. Ron's Trudes graced the shop from then on.

The flies known as Chuck's Trudes began on the front porch of a private clubhouse on the rough, brawling waters of the lower McCloud River, where some angling friends of mine were assembled. While my friends pounded the river, I set up the vise in the partial shade of the tall oaks and pines. I needed something that would float in that water. I tied a Trude, with an underbody of hollow hair to add bulk and flotation, and a sparse, flared wing; both ideas garnered from other flies that I was in the habit of tying.

The fly worked. The sparse, flared wing solved casting and delivery problems often associated with Trudes, while offering a more natural wing silhouette over a full, juicy looking herl body. To distinguish it from fuller winged, standard Trudes, the fly was called Chuck's Trude by my friends. On subsequent trips to the McCloud, other Trude patterns came into being. The Hare's Ear Trude and Yellow Trude were also first tied on that same porch at the clubhouse.

When I moved to Montana's Bitterroot Valley, the Trudes made the move with me, and were further refined and modified to their present form.

The Hare's Ear Trude answers the need for a nondescript downwing searching pattern, while the Yellow Trude is "close enough" to many of the yellow stonefly species that populate virtually every Western river.

The Hare's Ear can be tied in olive, amber or rust variations quite effectively, although the natural color works well most of the time. In a variety of sizes it can simulate everything from spruce moths to fluttering caddis. Don't forget the Krystal Flash rib, which segments the fly.

The Yellow Trude can be tied with everything from a golden amber body in the larger sizes, to chartreuse (eliminate the fluorescent tag) in a sixteen.

With all of these flies, keep the body silhouette full and the wing sparse. Don't be afraid to cook up your own variations to match the insects in your area.

CHUCK'S HARE'S EAR TRUDE

HOOK:	Tiemco 5212 or equivalent, sizes 8-16
THREAD:	3/0 or 6/0 gray or tan; thread size depends on hook size
TAIL / UNDERBODY:	Natural deer hair; fine back hair with long black tips preferred
BODY:	Hare's ear and Antron mixed
RIB:	Krystal Flash mixed color
WING:	White calf tail
HACKLE:	One grizzly hackle one Spencer golden ginger dyed grizzly

CHUCK'S YELLOW TRUDE

HOOK:	Tiemco 5212 or equivalent, sizes 10-16
THREAD:	6/0 fluorescent flame red for rear, 6/0 or 8/0 paleyellow for remainder of fly
TAIL:	Natural deer hair; fine back hair with long black tips preferred
BODY:	Yellow fine poly dubbing
WING:	White calf tail
HACKLE:	Grizzly neck hackle

CHUCK'S PEACOCK TRUDE

HOOK:	Tiemco 5212 or equivalent, sizes 8-12
THREAD:	3/0 or 6/0 black or dark olive
TAIL / UNDERBODY:	Natural deer hair, fine back hair with long black tips preferred
BODY:	Peacock herl
WING:	White calf tail
HACKLE:	Two Spencer grizzly saddles, one dyed Green Drake, one dyed Golden Ginger

Cal Bird Dubbing Tool

1. Wrap 2/3 of the hook shank with thread. Even tips on cleaned deer hair for the tail.

2. Tie in deer hair tail, secure by pinching with the thumb and index finger as shown. Clip the butt ends. The tail length is 1/3 shank length. Glue underbody.

3. Cut the tips from several strands of peacock herl. Note the proportion of the underbody in the background.

4. Tie in the peacock herl strands by the tips above the hook point.

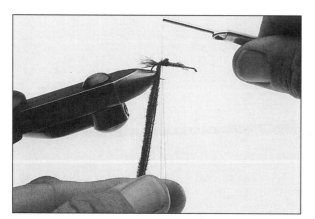

5. Form a dubbing loop with the thread.

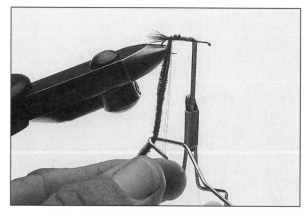

6. Hook the peacock herl with the Cal Bird dubbing tool catching the thread loop with the point of the tool.

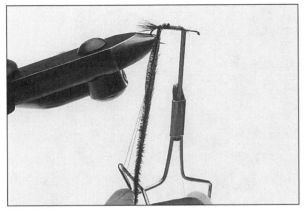

7. Bring the herl back against the thread. Keep the herl taut with the thumb and index finger of the left hand (thumb just below point of tool in photo).

8. Twist the tool with tension on the herl. This forms herl chenille with the thread.

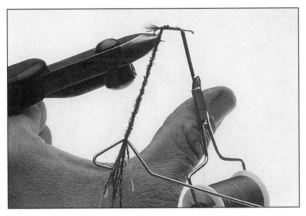

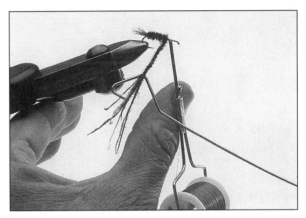

9. Tool positioned to now wrap the body.

10. Wrap the body to 1/3 back from the eye. Tie off and trim tag ends of the herl.

11. Select calf tail for the wing.

12. After evening tips of the sparse bunch of calf tail, position for length to the end of the tail.

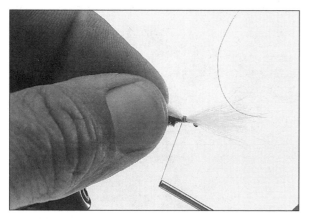

13. Secure in front of the body with thread wraps.

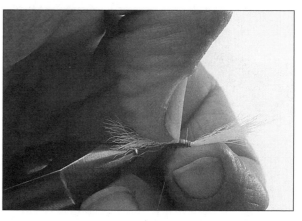

14. Flare the wing laterally by pressing down with the thumbnail as shown and securing with thread wraps.

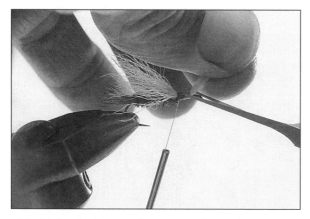

15. Trim the butt ends at an angle as shown.

16. Attach saddle hackles and wrap thread over the cut calf tail butts to form a taper as shown.

17. Hackle forward, tie off, clip the feather and whip finish.

18. Finished Chuck's Peacock Trude.

SEDUCER

Randall Kaufmann

The Seducer is a variation of the Stimulator and was originally designed to more closely imitate smaller stoneflies, including the *Isoperla patricia* and *Isoperla mormona*.

This pattern is commonly tied in yellows, greens and black in sizes 10-18. The material, Fly Wings, manufactured by Umpqua Feather Merchants, lends itself nicely to stonefly wings. It also makes wonderful caddis wings and is available in several colors. I add a couple of strands of Krystal Flash under the wing for sparkle.

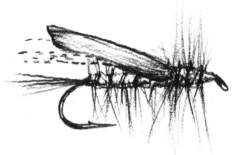

Some modifications can be made to make this fly more productive for certain fishing situations. When fishing to selective trout in slow water, trim the underside of the hackle flat or in a ' V ', allowing the fly to ride flush on the water surface. The addition of an elk hair wing over the top of the Fly Wings wing is useful for fast choppy water. Spread the hair wing wide and also spread the tail for better balance.

The Seducer can double for hoppers and caddis, or as a general purpose attractor on streams or lakes. It was so new that it was a last minute addition to my book, *Tying Dry Flies*. It proved successful in the summer of 1992 as a general purpose attractor on the Upper Colorado near Grandby, and on both the Arkansas and S. Fork of the Platte Rivers in Colorado. It also produced good numbers of cutthroat trout in the Lamar, Soda Butte, Clark's Fork, Yellowstone and Snake in Wyoming. During the Little Yellow Stone hatch on the Deschutes River, it is ' the fly '. Tied in black it is also an excellent winter stonefly imitation for dark stones.

Tie an assorted selection of sizes and colors of Seducers. They will liven up your fly box and give you plenty of angling action.

SEDUCER

HOOK:	Tiemco 200R, 5263, Dai-Riki 710 or equivalent, sizes 8-18
THREAD:	6/0 or 8/0 fluorescent orange
TAIL:	Moose body hair
RIBBING:	Fine gold wire
BODY:	Haretron dubbing in black, yellow, orange, green, tan, red, fluorescent colors and bright colors
BODY HACKLE:	Neck or saddle hackle in colors such as: dun, black, badger, grizzly, etc.
UNDERWING:	2-6 strands of Krystal Flash to complement the fly color (pearl is universal)
OVERWING:	Fly Film or Fly Wing (double over for sizes 8-12)
THORAX:	Fluorescent fire orange Antron, or peacock herl on Black Seducer
FOREHACKLE:	Grizzly saddle or other contrasting color saddle hackle

1. Lay down a thread base the full shank length. Attach the moose hair tail and make a full length underbody as shown. Extends one hook gape beyond the bend.

2. Attach fine gold wire to the far side of the hook.

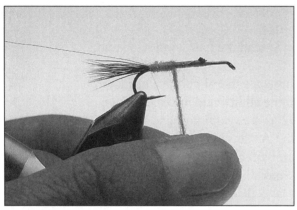

3. Dub from the tail to the thorax.

4. Attach hackle on top of the hook with the shiny side away from the tier.

5. Palmer the hackle back to the tail. Rib forward with the fine wire to secure the hackle.

6. After trimming hackle on the top of the fly, attach 2 to 6 strands of Krystal Flash as an underwing. Do not trim at this point.

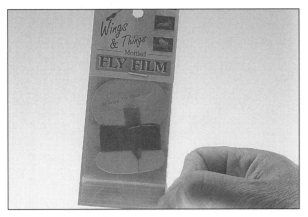

7. Use Fly Film for the wing material.

8. Cut the Fly Film wing to shape.

9. Tie in the wing 1/3 back from the eye. Cut the Krystal Flash to just beyond the wing. Wing extends only to mid-tail.

10. Attach the hackle at the 1/3 point. Dub in front of the hackle to the eye.

11. Hackle through the dubbed thorax, tie off, trim the tag of feather and whip finish.

12. Finished Seducer.

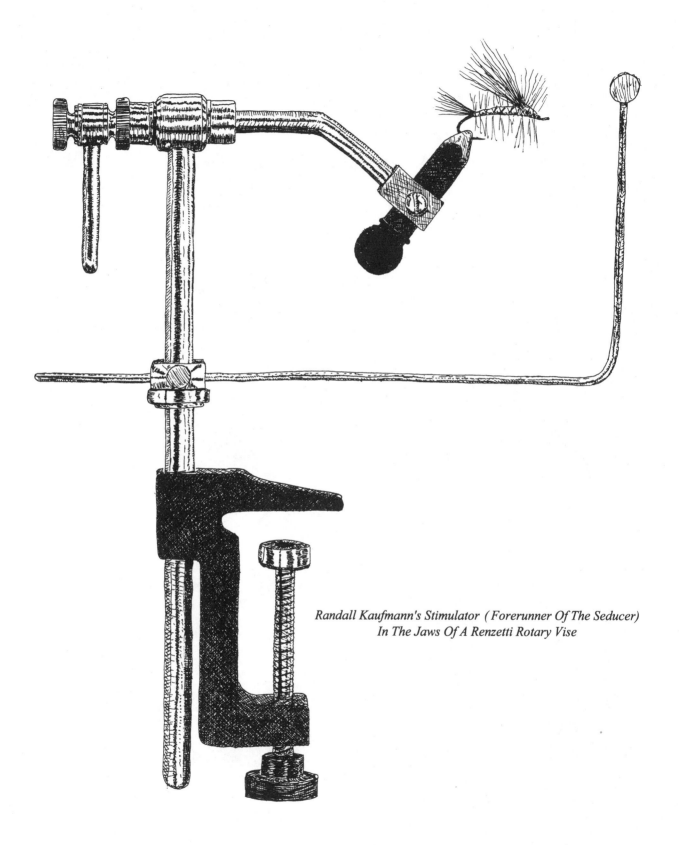

Randall Kaufmann's Stimulator (Forerunner Of The Seducer)
In The Jaws Of A Renzetti Rotary Vise

IMPROVED ROYAL HUMPY

Jack Dennis

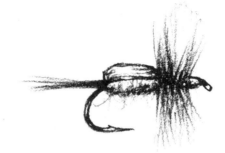

Since I first tied the Royal Humpy in the 1960's, I have continued to experiment with it. It is a fly that I featured in both of my previous fly tying books. I joke to people that by Volume II, I had learned how to tie the Royal Humpy the right way. Since publishing *Volume II* in 1980, I have discovered many new variations to the standard Royal Humpy.

The Royal Humpy can be tied with a variety of different hairs, the most popular of which is deer hair. For years our experimentation was limited by the type and color of deer hair we could obtain. Whitetails tended to have stiffer hair and to be more brown in color, while mule deer hair was thicker in diameter and tended to be a darker gray. Elk hair was either light or dark and was popular for wings. That limitation changed when a cold dyeing process was found which did not damage the hair, allowing us to have a variety of colors. This process also allowed the multi-shaded characteristics to show through, which gives a more realistic appearance of the venation or mottling in insect wings.

The dyeing process for grizzly hackle has also broadened the scope of variations in tying Humpies and Royal Humpies, as well as other flies. Mike Lawson confided in me that he felt the dyeing process made it possible for him to tie an effective Green Drake Wulff.

I feel that the addition of dubbing to the underbody of the Royal Humpy is the most innovative change since I first tied the pattern. It gives the fly a more buggy appearance and also helps it float better. It goes hand-in-hand with coordinating all the rest of the fly parts in a proper color scheme. A Green Drake Royal Humpy, for example, has an olive deer hair back, olive to gold dubbed underbody, olive dyed grizzly hackle and a black or white calf tail wing. Think of the color scheme you need to tie more realistic imitations of the naturals where you fish, and it won't be hard to tie a Royal Humpy to order.

The final thing I have learned to do over the years is to tie Humpies and Royal Humpies in much smaller sizes. By small, I mean sizes 18 through 24. At first this will sound intimidating to you, but if you follow a few simple rules and practice, you can tie any hair pattern in small sizes. Proportioning is the key; use small amounts of material and don't make either the wings or tail too long. A fly tying magnifier is very helpful for smaller flies.

With all the different materials available today, be creative when tying your Humpies and Royal Humpies. Let your imagination go and I know the results will follow.

IMPROVED ROYAL HUMPY

HOOK:	Dai-Riki 300, 305 or equivalent, sizes 10-22
THREAD:	6/0 waxed sizes 10 & 12; 8/0 waxed sizes 14-22
TAIL:	Moose hair
WING:	White calf body hair, or calf tail
BODY:	Olive dyed deer hair
UNDERBODY:	Olive Scintilla Dubbing
HACKLE:	Olive dyed Spencer grizzly saddle or neck hackle

1. Lay down a thread base for the tail.

2. Tie in a stacked moose hair tail about mid-shank. Tail extends one hook shank past the bend. Wrap thread forward to 1/3 from the eye.

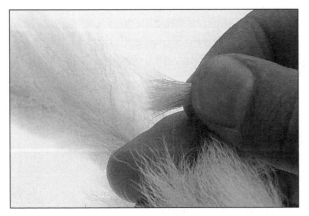

3. Select a bunch of calf tail and even the tips for the wing.

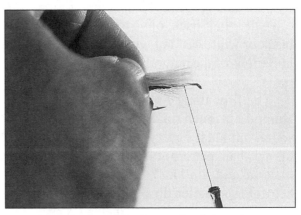

4. Measure the calf tail to a shank length.

5. Tie in calf tail on to the top of the hook at the 1/3 tie in point.

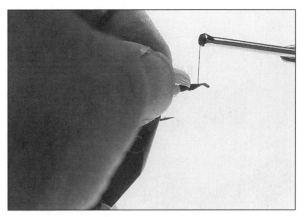

6. Make thread wraps in front of the calf tail to stand it up.

7. Trim the butts of the calf tail.

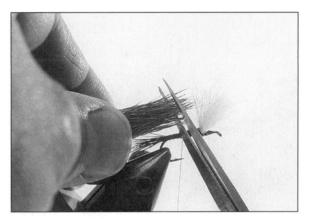

8. Trim the tips of the cleaned dyed deer hair as shown.

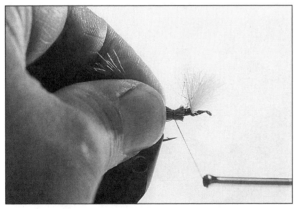

9. Tie in the deer hair by the trimmed tips just above the hook point.

10. Select a sparkling synthetic dubbing for the body.

11. Dub the body to mid-shank.

12. Divide the calf tail with the fingers and separate with the thread into a right and left side.

13. Make thread wraps around each individual wing to secure.

14. Pull the butts of the deer hair forward to form a back. Tie down behind the wings keeping the hair on top of the shank as you do so.

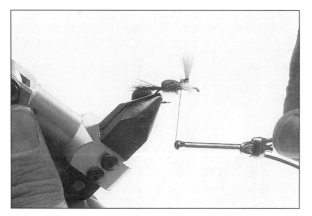

15. Shows the hair hump tied down behind the wing with the butts trimmed.

16. Tie in a grizzly saddle hackle behind the wing and hackle forward with equal wraps behind and in front of the wing.

17. Tie off and trim the hackle stem. Whip finish.

18. Finished Improved Royal Humpy.

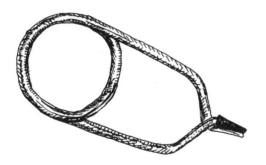

Veniard English Hackle Pliers

Griffin's Hair Stacker

DOUBLE HUMPY

Jack Dennis

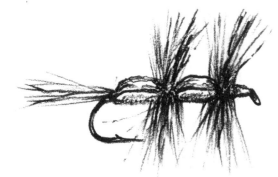

If one Humpy is good, two are better. So thought Joe Allen of Jackson Hole, Wyoming. Joe has lived in Jackson Hole all his life and has guided for most of his years on the Snake River. His pattern, the Double Humpy is simply two Humpies tied on the same long shank hook.

The Double Humpy can be tied in sizes 4 through 12 with sizes 6 and 8 being the most common choice. A variety of colors can be used for the underbody but yellow and red are the most common. An orange underbody of silk or poly yarn is very successful during the *Pteronarcys* stonefly hatch. When tied with lemon yellow in one segment and lime green in the other, it is affectionately called the Uncola Double Humpy, and it is quite effective. The Double Humpy can be tied with or without wings. Grizzly hackle is one critical material on this fly and should not be substituted with another choice of colors.

In addition to representing a stonefly, the Double Humpy may also be taken by the trout as a large caddis, grasshopper or cicada. Although it is most often fished dead drift, some guides tell their clients to pull it underwater. This does elicit some hardy strikes.

In the 1990 Jackson Hole One Fly, Tom Gould of Des Moines, Iowa used a Double Humpy to edge out Curt Gowdy by one quarter inch, catching the largest trout in the event. Tom, whose boatmate for the day was Joan Wulff, landed a 21 1/4" cutthroat. Many other anglers in the 1990 event tallied good scores using the Double Humpy.

DOUBLE HUMPY

HOOK:	Mustad 9672, Dai-Riki 710 or equivalent, sizes 4-12
THREAD:	Yellow flat waxed nylon
TAIL:	Natural deer body hair
BACKS & WINGS:	Natural deer body hair
BODY:	Yellow poly yarn, 4 strand floss, or tying thread
HACKLE:	2 to 4 grizzly saddle or neck hackles

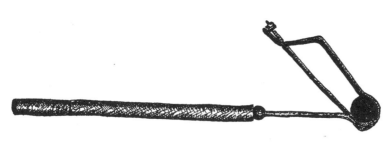

Griffin's Rotary Hackle Pliers

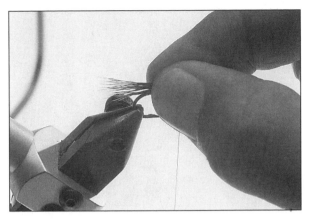

1. Tie in the deer hair tail about 1 1/2 gaps beyond the bend of the hook.

2. Tie the deer hair for the rear hump of the fly with tips extending a shank length beyond the bend.

3. Tie in poly yarn to be used for the body. Notice that all materials have been tied in at the same point to form an even underbody.

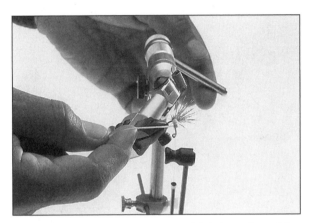

4. Wrap the poly yarn body, which is easier with a rotary vise.

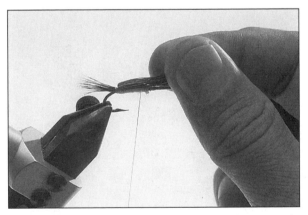

5. Pull the deer hair forward forming a hump and tie down to form a flared hair wing.

6. Select a pair of neck hackles for the rear hackle.

283

7. Tie in the hackle behind the wing and wrap the hackles behind and in front of the wing.

8. After standing the rear wing up with thread and hackle wraps select a shank length of clean, stacked deer hair for the forward hump and wing.

9. Tie in the front wing material 1/4 back from the eye and wrap the thread back to the rear wing. Tie in poly yarn and wrap forward body segment.

10. Pull the deer hair forward forming a hump and tie down flaring the forward wing.

11. Hackle in the same manner as you did in the rear section and whip finish.

12. Finished Double Humpy.

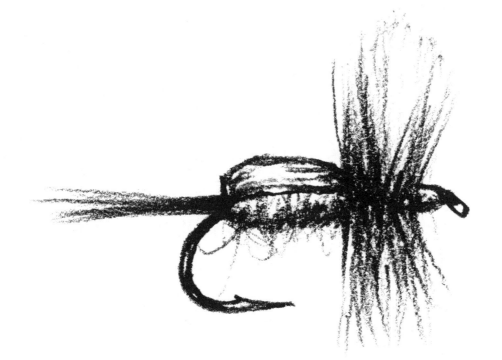

INDEX

INDEX

INDEX